At last! A sane and sensitive book on emotion in the Christian life, an area where extremes prevail and balance is rare. There is something of huge value here both for touchy-feely believers and Christians who have scarcely allowed themselves to touch an emotion in years – as well as everyone in between. The section about ministry and emotion is especially valuable.
Julian Hardyman, Senior Pastor, Eden Baptist Church, Cambridge

For much of the last century, psychologists and psychiatrists focused on 'bad' feelings, like depression and anxiety: the language of dis-ease and what makes us 'ill'. Only recently have we begun to explore the world of positive emotion: the language of joy, gratitude, optimism and what makes us 'well'. In the same way, church teaching has often focused on the pain, conflict and dangers that lurk in human emotions, but neglected the positive side of human flourishing. Graham Beynon's book, an important corrective full of practical wisdom, introduces us to the whole kaleidoscopic range of emotions that lie at the very centre of what it means to be made in the image of God himself. As well as furnishing us with a balanced and accessible pastoral resource, this book is another challenge to the recovery of biblical preaching that reaches the whole person: the 'heart' as well as the 'head'.
Glynn Harrison, Emeritus Professor of Psychiatry, University of Bristol

In a field prone to controversy and extreme attitudes, Graham Beynon has written an admirably balanced book. Solidly founded on a biblical framework of emotions, this provides a very practical approach to the place of feelings in everyday life, and, in particular, in our Christian experience. I cannot think of a better book to help us understand, appreciate, and recover the value and the joy of emotions.
Pablo Martinez, psychiatrist, Bible teacher and author

This is neither theological treatise nor pop psychology but a highly readable book where Graham brings a biblical mind and a pastor's heart to this ever-present subject. Looking at emotions in this way fills a useful gap in the market.
Auriel Schluter, pastoral counsellor

Biblical Christianity no longer means leaving your brain at the door. Not only are logic and reason welcome, but here emotions and your heart are too. Learning from Jesus, this book explains how emotions affect how we sing, serve and even study God's Word. It challenges both quick answers and poor theology, explores stigma and encourages warmth. In today's reactive culture it brings a clear model and suggests helpful steps to take.
Dr Rob Waller, consultant psychiatrist, a Director of www. mindandsoul.info and author of The Worry Book

emotions

emotions

emotions
living life in colour

graham beynon

INTER-VARSITY PRESS
Norton Street, Nottingham NG7 3HR, England
Email: ivp@ivpbooks.com
Website: www.ivpbooks.com

First published 2012

British Library Cataloguing in Publication Data
A catalogue record for this book is available from the British Library.

ISBN: 978-1-84474-589-0

Set in Dante 12/15pt
Typeset in Great Britain by CRB Associates, Potterhanworth, Lincolnshire
Printed and bound in Great Britain by Ashford Colour Press Ltd, Gosport,
Hampshire

*Inter-Varsity Press publishes Christian books that are true to the Bible and that
communicate the gospel, develop discipleship and strengthen the church for its
mission in the world.*

*Inter-Varsity Press is closely linked with the Universities and Colleges Christian
Fellowship, a student movement connecting Christian Unions in universities and
colleges throughout Great Britain, and a member movement of the International
Fellowship of Evangelical Students. Website: www.uccf.org.uk*

To Simon and Mandy,
faithful friends over many years

contents

preface

I think of people's faces showing emotion:

- Debbie's face shining with happiness and delight
- Alan's face hard with cold fury
- Estelle's face sad and tired from crying
- Brian's face gloriously triumphant
- Gregory's face full of happy satisfaction
- Rosalyn's face bitter with disappointment
- Julie's face despairing and confused
- Joe's face relaxed and contented

All people I know, all people feeling feelings.

* * *

God made us to feel. Feelings were his idea in the first place. But they bring us both heartache and joy, confusion and satisfaction. They can seem mysterious, uncontrollable, unreliable. When they are good, we love them; when they are bad, we would prefer not to have them. But life without feelings wouldn't be life as God made it, life in colour.

A conversation some years ago got me thinking about the place of emotions in the Christian life. What we should feel, and what we shouldn't, and what we can and can't do about it. It has been a journey of exploration into the Bible, into the writings of church history, into modern thought, and into my own emotions. This book is the result of where my thinking has got to, which is not as far as I would have liked, but I hope it is far enough to be helpful to you.

As is the case with all I have written, I am indebted to others: all those I've read on the topic, many of whom are referenced, but some not; all those I've talked to on the topic who have shaped my thinking; all those who've listened to teaching I've given and have taken the time to feed back. Thank you, one and all.

Thanks particularly to those who took the time to read a draft of this book and feed back helpful comments – this is a better book as a result. Those kind people were: Sandra Byatt, Gordon Dalzell, Julian Hardyman, Ed Moll, Richard Perkins, Auriel Schluter, Christine Sherwood, Louise Silk and Dave Tricker. Thanks also to my Editor Eleanor Trotter who has been unfailingly encouraging and wise in her guidance.

I should also mention that various individuals' stories appear in the following chapters as examples. I have drawn on different sources for these and have changed names and various details, and on occasion have merged stories together. That is both to hide identities and to make the stories helpful within the flow of the book. I trust they will still reflect the real people behind them.

It is my hope and prayer that this book will help you to feel as God made you to feel.

Graham Beynon
March 2012

part 1
understanding emotions

1
approaching emotions

'How are you?' people ask. We reply that we're well or tired, happy or sad. We might talk about enjoying time with family, or feeling satisfied with something at work. Or maybe that we're annoyed by a neighbour or frustrated with our football team. We answer the how-are-you question with facts about what's going on in our life, but the real answer is about how we're feeling inside.

Just think about the range of things we feel. Here's my list:

Desire	Pride	Admiration
Hope	Sorrow	Jealousy
Grief	Suspicion	Anger
Contempt	Humility	Envy
Contentment	Embarrassment	Compassion
Love	Reverence	Awe
Fear	Adoration	Anxiety
Wonder	Pity	Surprise

Assurance	Peace	Elation
Concern	Sympathy	Fondness
Revulsion	Regret	Delight
Happiness	Hatred	Joy
Shame	Satisfaction	Worry
Dislike	Despair	Remorse

And that's not all of them!

Emotions are part of everyday life. More than that, they're a hugely significant part of everyday life. A life of pure facts would be pretty dull. As we do our work, live in our families, pursue our hobbies and spend time with our friends, we feel things. That's what makes life enjoyable or exasperating, fun or frustrating. Facts are black and white; feelings mean we live life in colour.

You could even say that what we feel is more important than the facts themselves. Imagine you had the choice between having a long-term illness, but feeling at peace about it and still satisfied with life, versus being physically well but being discontented. Which would you choose? Or how about being short of money, but still enjoying life on a budget, versus being loaded but bored? Circumstances and feelings are often connected, but how we feel about life is often more important to us than what is going on in life.

That's because feelings bring colour to life – both dark and light shades. Living with negative emotions of sadness, frustration, bitterness or angst is an awful life, no matter how healthy or wealthy we might be. Whereas feelings of happiness, satisfaction, contentment and peace are part of a pleasant life, even if we suffer hardships.

Emotions are huge too in their influence upon us. Think of the choices we make: what work we do, how we spend our money, which hobbies we take up, how we spend time with friends. Lots of things come into play, but a massive part is how we feel about things, or how we think those things will make us feel.

Emotions are part of life and they are a hugely significant part of life.

An emotional world

As I was growing up, there was a character in the TV series *Star Trek* who was called Spock. He was from the planet Vulcan. He was the master of logical thought: everything was based on facts and analysed without the complicating involvement of emotions. His standard reply 'to decisions of his human captain was, 'But Captain, that's not logical.' (We later find out that Vulcans have strong emotions but keep them tightly under control!)

A later character on *Star Trek*, called Data, was an android who was also very logical, but programmed at least to understand and take account of basic human emotions. However, he is later fitted with an 'emotion chip' and realizes his dream of being more fully human. But today on *Star Trek* you won't find such a logical character. People speak about how they feel and what they sense; they rely on memories and intuition. Logic is out, feelings are in.

We live in an increasingly 'emotional' world. Adverts are rarely designed to give us information; instead they try to make us feel something. BMW used to try to convince you that their cars were the 'ultimate driving machine', but now they advertise with just one word: 'joy'.

Of course it's not that we never used to care about feelings, and today we are naturally still concerned with facts and logical thought – especially if it has to do with mending the car or our finances. But our culture as a whole gives a much higher place to feelings than it used to. Think about how people speak about their decisions: 'It felt right'; 'I had a good feeling about it'; 'If it feels good, do it.'

We are also a culture that *wants* to feel things. We want positive emotions like happiness and fulfilment. Popular self-help books used to advertise that they would help you become successful; now they say they'll help you become happy. Rather than aiming at certain achievements, we aim at certain feelings.

Our culture has also become more emotionally expressive. The Brits used to be known for not showing their feelings – indeed crying was a sign of weakness. I'm not saying that's all gone, but it's more usual now to think that we should let every emotion out.

Reality TV and talent shows are obvious examples. Barely a week of *X-Factor* goes by without someone finding it all too much, breaking down and crying. In fact if you don't break down at some point, you'll be thought of as a bit distant and not caring – it certainly won't help your voting figures. In days gone by, people would have looked down on those who felt deeply and showed it in tears; today you're more likely to be looked down on for remaining cool, calm and collected. Christians can't escape their culture, and so we shouldn't be surprised that we are being influenced by it all.

An emotional Christian world?

When we think about emotions in the Christian life, a whole variety of other issues pop up. How should we feel in our relationship with God? Does being a Christian mean I shouldn't feel certain things like anger or frustration? Should I trust my feelings as a Christian? What should I do if I don't feel anything at all?

Here's a variety of what people say and struggle with:

'What really matters is truth – you can't trust your feelings. You just have to believe what is right and forget about how you feel.'

'You can't control your emotions, can you? You feel how you feel and you just have to live with it.'

'You have to follow your feelings – how else can you be true to yourself?'

'I know doing this is wrong, but I can't deny how I feel.'

'There's a huge gap between what I think and feel – I know stuff is true about God but I don't feel anything.'

'I can't stop feeling so angry – it's controlling me.'

'I'm overwhelmed by the feeling of God's love; it floods my heart and I feel like I'm going to burst.'

'I'm always anxious. I know I should trust God but I just can't stop myself worrying.'

'If only I could feel like God actually loved me!'

All these statements were made by Christians – about their feelings.

Feelings are a particular issue for Christians. Some feel controlled by their emotions and want to break free from them. Others long for more emotion: wanting to know more of God's love or peace. Some resign themselves to whatever they happen to feel. Others wrestle with their feelings, seeking change.

The famous minister Martyn Lloyd-Jones said,

> I suppose that one of the greatest problems in our life in this world, not only for Christians, but for all people, is the right handling of our feelings and emotions. Oh, the havoc that is wrought, and the tragedy, the misery and the wretchedness that are to be found in the world, simply because people do not know how to handle their own feelings![1]

Emotions – good or bad?

Christians have had trouble making up their minds about emotions. Sometimes we see them as great – usually when we're feeling good. Sometimes we see them as terrible – usually when we're struggling.

Overall, the negative view has been the loudest voice down through the years. There has been a consistent trend in the Christian world to downplay feelings and see them as dangerous, misleading and unhelpful. At times we have implied that God would have been better off making us without emotions. That's meant that many people have thought they shouldn't talk about their feelings, often resulting in them shoving them deep inside themselves and exhibiting an unhealthy head-only type of faith.

But 'emotions are good' has occasionally appeared too. Sometimes it's been feelings in the context of worship as people have experienced God in a new way, or feelings of God's love and presence, or a focus on how much we love God or care for other people.

Think about the differences shown in figure 1.

When emotion is everything

The left-hand column represents emotions as everything. We think emotions are a significant and an important part of life.

Feelings are to be followed	OR	Feelings are to be ignored
Feelings are to be sought	OR	Feelings are to be suppressed
Feelings are to be trusted	OR	Feelings are to be questioned
Feelings are significant	OR	Feelings are insignificant
Feelings are controlling	OR	Feelings can be controlled

Figure 1

We seek out emotions, and we're concerned about how we feel. We may worry if we don't feel very much when we think we should. We think with our feelings, believing what they tell us is true even if we 'think' something else. How we feel guides the decisions we make. We assess our spiritual life by how we feel.

When emotion is nothing

The right-hand column represents emotions as nothing. We focus on what we should think and do, and emotions aren't very important to us. We don't spend much time reflecting on how we feel. We might be surprised that we feel a particular emotion, but then we press on regardless. We certainly never follow a feeling or trust what it is telling us. We're more likely to assess our spiritual condition by what we believe and what we do.

Of course I'm describing opposite ends of a spectrum, but you may still recognize elements of these in yourself, and most people would place themselves more in one group than the other. Just so you know where I'm coming from, with my background I would fit more in the 'emotion-is-nothing' group, but give me a poignant moment in a film with some decent background music and I'll be weeping with the best of them. Which just goes to show that most of us are really a bit of a mixture.

Getting our bearings

You may immediately say that these differences between us are simply because we have different personalities, some of us being more 'emotional' than others. And I agree. But this still raises huge questions about what we should think of emotions and what role they should play in our lives. Should we forget about them and focus on truth? Should we seek them, and if so how, and should we follow them? Whatever our personality type, there are questions we need to answer and potential changes we need to make.

First, while we might describe some people as 'emotional' and others as 'logical', actually everyone is emotional to some extent. We all feel something about our life, our work, our faith, and our relationships and so on. To be utterly unfeeling is not to be human. In fact it's to deny part of how God has made us. We are created as thinking, feeling and acting beings, not as logical machines. So while we may vary in how deeply we feel things, we all do feel!

Additionally, we need to see that the Christian life as described in the Bible is full of feelings. The apostle Paul says to the Philippians that he is working for their 'progress and joy in the faith' (Philippians 1:25). Now that really struck me. In fact that was roughly where my search into all this started. I was happy enough speaking about someone's 'progress' in the faith – their growth in understanding and maturity – but Paul also adds 'joy'. Paul wanted to see joy in people's lives. In fact that's part of what he was working for.

> *To be utterly unfeeling is not to be human.*

Later in the same letter, Paul gives the command to 'rejoice in the Lord always' (Philippians 4:4). The joy and rejoicing he's talking about here are more solid things than fleeting feelings of happiness, but they still involve how we feel. We'll return to how you can *command* an emotion later on, but for now just notice that for Paul growth and obedience in the Christian life is about more than knowledge and behaviour.

Seeing that got me noticing other areas of 'emotion'. Paul speaks about people 'overflowing with thankfulness' (Colossians 2:7). Which presumably involves some level of *feeling* thankful!

He also speaks about 'godly sorrow' which leads to repentance (2 Corinthians 7:10). He contrasts this with 'worldly sorrow' which leads to death. That means we can feel bad about our sin in a right or a wrong way. Our sorrow can be 'godly' or 'worldly'. In which case, I need to know how I should feel.

Or Jesus tells his disciples, 'Do not worry' (Matthew 6:25–34). So he expects them to experience 'peace'. In that passage, the peace Jesus talks about involves believing the truth about God's care, but it also involves not feeling worried!

Paul also speaks about contentment, in Philippians 4:11–13 and 1 Timothy 6:6–10. Again, truth is involved: it means not believing certain things about money and circumstances, which Paul explains. It also means that my heart doesn't have a constant longing for what I don't have, but rather contentment with what I do have. In other words, it involves feelings.

Deeper heart attitudes

We can also think about some deeper heart attitudes. Think of Jesus' words about the most important commandment: 'Love the Lord your God with all your heart and with all your soul and with all your mind and with all your strength' (Mark 12:30). This love of God involves obedience to God's law. Any amount of loving feeling towards God that doesn't show itself in an obedient life is meaningless. But obedience while feeling cold towards God isn't right either. In fact, if we do the 'right thing' but have no heart for God at all, the danger is that our faith becomes external. In other words, this love of God must have an element of feeling in it.

Then think of what Jesus says is the second most important commandment: 'Love your neighbour as yourself' (Mark 12:31). Again, this must show itself in loving actions, otherwise it's just lip service – which John condemns as useless (1 John 3:18). However, to do the act lovingly towards people while hating their guts isn't right either! Theologian Don Carson says about love between Christians: 'The command to love must not be stripped of its affective component.'[2] In other words, it must involve some amount of feeling.

The same is true of other attitudes we're supposed to have towards one another. Paul says:

> Therefore, as God's chosen people, holy and dearly loved, clothe yourselves with compassion, kindness, humility, gentleness and patience. Bear with each other and forgive one another if any of you has a grievance against someone. Forgive as the Lord forgave you. And over all these virtues put on love, which binds them all together in perfect unity.
> (Colossians 3:12–14)

Being compassionate and patient and forgiving people are very much attitudes we have towards one another that show themselves in how we act. But they also involve how we feel. You can't forgive someone and then carry on feeling resentment and bitterness towards them. You can't be patient with someone while boiling with rage because of their annoying habits.

In other words, while these deeper heart attitudes are much, much more than an emotion, they do contain an emotional element.

Blurred boundaries

What we're starting to wrestle with now are the muddy waters of what an emotion is. In one sense it's obvious: it is something that we feel. But the boundaries are very blurred. There is what we could call a 'pure' emotion, like surprise at something startling, or awe at something impressive. We have little control over these; they are automatic responses and are usually quite brief – it's hard to remain surprised for very long!

Then there are recognizable feelings like joy, peace, thankfulness or contentment. These are longer lasting; we might think of them as a 'mood'. We have more control over them because they involve our thoughts and beliefs. For example, Paul speaks about 'giving joyful thanks to the Father, who has qualified you to share in the inheritance of his holy people in the kingdom of light' (Colossians 1:12). Which means that I should feel joy because I know and believe God has done these things, and I value how good God has been to me in rescuing me. So this isn't 'bare emotion'; these feelings flow from my beliefs and what my heart values. (We'll be coming back to this idea a lot.)

Lastly, there are attitudes like love, compassion, humility and patience. These are more character traits than moods, but they involve some element of how we feel.

You can't have them and not have some element of feeling. You certainly can't have these heart attitudes and at the same time have the opposite feeling, for example be humble but still feel self-important.

So it's messy, and that messiness will continue through this book. In one sense, this shouldn't surprise us. We are made as whole people, thinking, feeling and acting. We can't, or shouldn't, divide ourselves up into different compartments.

Dangers ahead

Dividing ourselves up actually opens the door to two key dangers. The first is being hypocrites. It is not enough for us to know about God, speak for God, and even act for God. That can be done by hypocrites who don't actually love God. It is the danger of an external faith that feels nothing for God.

This was one of the dangers that some of the Pharisees fell into. Jesus sometimes criticized their understanding and their actions, but more often he went for their hearts. For example:

> He replied, 'Isaiah was right when he prophesied about you hypocrites; as it is written:
>
> "These people honour me with their lips,
>   but their hearts are far from me."'
> (Mark 7:6)

Here's a group saying the right thing, and often doing the right thing, but their hearts are far from God. I'm not saying that they just needed some emotion. The heart attitude Jesus is talking about is a much more substantial thing, but it did involve feelings towards God. If we don't think through the right place for emotions in our lives, then we too could be in danger of the same words of rebuke from Jesus.

But the second danger is the possibility of empty emotion. It's not enough either simply to have deep feelings for God or great experiences of God. That can even be the case for people who don't really know God at all. It is the danger of an emotional faith that fails to understand God.

The apostle Paul wrote about a group a bit like this in his letter to the Colossians, a group that was having some great experiences of God, presumably involving great feeling. Here is Paul's response: 'Do not let anyone who delights in false humility and the worship of angels disqualify you. Such a person also goes into great detail about what they have seen; they are puffed up with idle notions by their unspiritual mind' (Colossians 2:18). These people's great experience actually indicates nothing about their spirituality. In fact Paul calls them unspiritual. There's nothing good or helpful about experience and emotion by itself when it has lost connection with Jesus.

There's nothing good or helpful about experience and emotion by itself when it has lost connection with Jesus.

Thinking, feeling, acting

To put all of this differently, we can think of three elements of our being. There is what we *think*, what we *feel* and what we *do*. We want all three of these acting together rightly. So my mind understands something about God – say his goodness to me in salvation. And that right understanding means that I feel thankful or joyful. And this will show itself in my choices and actions – I choose to live for God or praise him for his goodness. All three are present and all three are connected. My feelings of thankfulness are because of my understanding, and my actions flow from my understanding and feeling.

We need all three areas functioning in the Christian life. Let's think about some of the ways we can go wrong if one or more of these is missing:

Thinking only

This is just intellectual assent to truth. There may be great understanding, but no real conviction. It's like believing a fact that makes no difference to life – like that water is made up of oxygen and hydrogen. It's true, but it makes no impact on your life; you acknowledge it and then simply move on. That kind of knowledge of God is a dangerous thing. See James 2:17 where believing something without it affecting your actions is called 'dead'.

Feeling only

This is just empty emotionalism. There may be great depth of feeling but it doesn't come from any understanding of God or show itself in any obedience to God. This is like being moved by a film, but it's all because of the background music and soppy sentimentality. The next day you wonder why you felt so deeply.

Acting only

This is just doing the right thing. People obey, but not because of any understanding of God or a heart for God. This is like a child obeying a parent's instruction just because they say so – where there is no understanding or conviction about what he is doing. Religion becomes external and empty.

It should be clear by now that what we want is all three of these operating together. In fact, only all three being present is what we would call a real response to God. If someone says they understand God's goodness in salvation but feel nothing about it, then I would say they haven't really understood it at all. But similarly, if someone says they feel something very deeply but it doesn't show in their obedience, then it's just frothy emotion which has no substance. I want my thinking, feeling and acting integrated and working together so that I respond to God with all of my being.

The way forward

We've explored emotions and seen that they form a significant part of life, and hence the Christian life. They can't be ignored, suppressed or relegated. However, neither must they be given pride of place. Rather they must take their right place as part of our response to God and

I want my thinking, feeling and acting integrated and working together so that I respond to God with all of my being.

living out of relationship with God. We now need to examine more carefully what place that is and then think about how we start to live out this life.

Questions for reflection

1. What have you noticed about how our culture views feelings today?
2. What have you been taught as a Christian about emotions?
3. Do you tend towards thinking of emotions as good or bad? Why?
4. Do you agree that the Christian life involves how we feel? Why or why not?
5. Which of the different dangers do you think you run the risk of?

2
what do perfect emotions look like?

What does a mature Christian feel? How should he or she respond emotionally to the ups and downs of life? In other words, what do we want our emotional life to look like? Let's begin by looking at Jesus.

The emotional life of Jesus
Jesus was (and is) fully man and fully God. He is the one and only 'God-man'. Right now though the point we want to emphasize is that he was a man – and that meant he both felt and expressed human emotions.

That might seem obvious, but it's still worth saying. We can very easily have a semi-spiritualized view of Jesus. We imagine him walking on water, but not sitting on the toilet. We think of his amazing miracles, but not enjoying a meal with friends. In other words, we forget how fully human Jesus was.

And Jesus, in his humanity, is an example to us. We often talk about this, saying we want to become more 'Christ-like'.

What we mean is that we want to be more like Jesus in his love, integrity, compassion and righteousness. And so we should! He is the one and only perfect model of what true humanity should look like, and every one of us is a twisted picture by comparison. So being the perfect example to us of what it means to be human, Jesus is also a perfect example in his emotional life.

I should add that Jesus as part of the Godhead also had an emotional life before becoming a man. There have been lots of debates about how God does and doesn't feel emotion. I think he does feel emotions, but not in the same way as we do. (I'm not going to examine that issue because our focus here is on *our* emotions, but you can follow it up in the recommended further reading at the back.)

Our focus for now is Jesus' emotional life once he'd become a man. Back in the nineteenth century a theologian called Benjamin Warfield wrote a paper called: 'The Emotional Life of Our Lord'. In it he looked through the Gospels and examined examples of where Jesus expressed emotion of one kind or another. We'll look at some of his examples below.

Jesus feeling compassionate

Compassion is the emotion that is most frequently attributed to Jesus. It can be sparked by a variety of situations, but often it is because of someone's illness. We read in Matthew that Jesus meets two blind men who call on him to heal them: 'Jesus had compassion on them and touched their eyes. Immediately they received their sight and followed him' (Matthew 20:34).

When Jesus saw blind or crippled or ill people he was moved. He felt something for that person and their situation.

Or Jesus can feel compassion because of a concern for what people might face. For example, after teaching a crowd for some time Jesus says this: 'I have compassion for these people; they have already been with me three days and have nothing to eat. If I send them home hungry, they will collapse on the way, because some of them have come a long distance' (Mark 8:2–3).

Jesus also has compassion on people who are experiencing tragedy. When walking into the town of Nain, he meets a woman who is a widow (presumably her husband had died a while ago), and now she is on her way to bury her only son. It's absolutely tragic:

> As he approached the town gate, a dead person was being carried
> out – the only son of his mother, and she was a widow. And a
> large crowd from the town was with her. When the Lord saw
> her, his heart went out to her and he said, 'Don't cry.'
> (Luke 7:12–13)

When Jesus saw this tragic situation, 'his heart went out' to that widow. Those words are actually a different translation of the same phrase we saw earlier – having compassion on someone – but it's a good way of expressing it. In seeing someone's tragedy, Jesus feels for them in his heart.

Jesus also has compassion on people's spiritual condition. In Matthew we read: 'When he saw the crowds, he had compassion on them, because they were harassed and helpless, like sheep without a shepherd' (Matthew 9:36). Jesus knows this is a group with no spiritual leadership, and so they are harassed and helpless. He feels for them.

So we see Jesus' heart filled with pity and concern. He doesn't remain indifferent to hardship and pain. Quite the opposite! When he sees them, he is filled with compassion – and it is right that he is. It would in fact have been wrong to have remained impassive and unmoved. Indeed, that would have been hard-hearted and callous. But Jesus shows us a right model of caring compassion.

Jesus feeling angry

Jesus also got angry with people. Of course he was right to do so. Just as the compassion above was right and appropriate, so was his anger. Paul tells us, 'In your anger do not sin' (Ephesians 4:26), which must mean we can be rightly as well as wrongly angry.

So when Jesus was going to heal someone on the Sabbath day, the religious leaders were there looking for a reason to accuse him. We read: 'He looked around at them in anger and, deeply distressed at their stubborn hearts, said to the man, "Stretch out your hand." He stretched it out, and his hand was completely restored' (Mark 3:5).

Jesus is not impressed. The Pharisees should have been concerned for the man with the shrivelled hand, and not looking to accuse him. Such attitudes flow from their stubborn hearts, and Jesus is angry with them and distressed about their wrong thoughts.

Jesus was also angry with his disciples. When people were bringing their children to him, the disciples took it upon themselves to stop them. When Jesus saw this, we're told 'he was indignant' (Mark 10:14). That's not such a strong word as we saw above, but he's still angry with them. And he's angry because what they were doing was wrong – he was right to be angry.

Jesus feeling sad

In some situations, Jesus expresses sadness or a deep distress. When Lazarus dies, Jesus is speaking with his sister Mary who is desperately upset. Here's how John describes the scene:

> When Jesus saw her weeping, and the Jews who had come along with her also weeping, he was deeply moved in spirit and troubled. 'Where have you laid him?' he asked.

'Come and see, Lord,' they replied.

Jesus wept.

Then the Jews said, 'See how he loved him!'

(John 11:33–36)

It's an emotionally charged scene: Jesus deeply moved and troubled by the sight of Mary's tears. And then, on seeing the tomb, Jesus weeps himself. Those watching can see that his sadness flows from his love for Lazarus.

We also see Jesus weep as he approaches Jerusalem. He knows that the people will reject him and that, as a result, God's judgment will fall on them. He knows that such judgment is good and right, but he takes no pleasure in it. And so we read that, as he 'approached Jerusalem and saw the city, he wept over it' (Luke 19:41). And he was right to do so.

Jesus feeling love

We saw above that, when Jesus wept for Lazarus, those watching said it was because he loved him so much. In fact earlier on in that account, a message is sent to Jesus about Lazarus's illness. It is phrased like this: 'So the sisters sent word to Jesus, "Lord, the one you love is sick"' (John 11:3).

Lazarus was someone with whom Jesus had a close relationship, such that he could be called 'the one Jesus loved'. Jesus of course loved everyone, but here we see that he had developed a closer affection for some than for others. Similarly, we read several times about the 'disciple whom Jesus loved' (e.g. John 13:23; 21:20).

We also see Jesus' love for other individuals. When a rich young man comes to him asking how to be saved, Jesus has to confront him with his love of money. He has to tell him some firm words about giving his money away, but the man loves his money too much and won't do it. Within that encounter, Mark gives us this telling insight: 'Jesus looked at him and loved him' (Mark 10:21). As Jesus looked him in the eye and told him what he needed to do, he felt a love for him.

Jesus feeling frustrated

On occasions Jesus got really fed up with people. Again this wasn't because he was impatient or bad-tempered. No, it was perfectly appropriate. For example: 'The Pharisees came and began to question Jesus. To test him, they asked him for a sign from heaven. He sighed deeply and said, "Why does this generation ask for a sign? Truly I tell you, no sign will be given to it"' (Mark 8:11–12).

Jesus is being tested by the Pharisees who won't believe in him – they've seen plenty of works and they should believe but instead they resist and demand more proof. Jesus' response is to 'sigh deeply'. That translation doesn't quite capture the essence. It has the sense of 'a deep groan from the heart'. He is frustrated and exasperated with them, and so he should be.

Jesus feeling joyful

Jesus also rejoices. On one occasion his disciples return from a preaching tour which has gone well, and Jesus responds like this: 'At that time Jesus, full of joy through the Holy Spirit, said, "I praise you, Father, Lord of heaven and earth, because you have hidden these things from the wise and learned, and revealed them to little children. Yes, Father, for this is what you were pleased to do"' (Luke 10:21). Jesus sees how God his Father has organized things – how he has revealed his salvation to people like his disciples who resemble children – and he rejoices in it. That joy bursts out onto his lips in a cry of praise.

Jesus feeling distress

We see Jesus' emotions most clearly and deeply just before his death. When he is praying in the Garden of Gethsemane, his feelings are expressed in very strong words: 'He took Peter, James and John along with him, and he began to be deeply distressed and troubled. "My soul is overwhelmed with sorrow to the point of death," he said to them. "Stay here and keep watch"' (Mark 14:33–34).

Jesus is saying that sorrow and sadness are like a flood over him. The anguish is so overwhelming that it's crushing him to death. And no wonder! Because Jesus knew what awaited him the next day – the horror of crucifixion where he would endure the wrath of his Father. And this was decision time. And so it was not only understandable but right that he felt such anguish. Notice though that Jesus feels deeply, but is not controlled by his feelings. He is in great distress about what God is calling him to do, but he will still go through with it. However, his commitment to God's plans doesn't mean he denies how he feels.

We could add more examples. Jesus speaks of his love for the Father (John 14:31), the tension he is under for his mission to be completed (Luke 12:50) and his longing and desire (Luke 22:15).

Fully feeling

What we see in Jesus is a fully functioning emotional life. Jesus feels deeply, and yet he always feels rightly. Here is Benjamin Warfield's summary of Jesus' feelings:

> Various as they are, they do not inhibit one another; compassion and indignation rise together in his soul; joy and sorrow meet in his heart and kiss each other. Strong as they are – not mere

joy but exultation, not mere irritated annoyance but raging indignation, not mere passing pity but the deepest movements of compassion and love, not mere surface distress but an exceeding sorrow even unto death – they never overmaster him. He remains ever in control.[1]

Jesus' heart contained different emotions, but they didn't override one another. Jesus' emotions were under control, that is, he never lost it. Jesus feels things, feels them deeply, and always rightly. So the Reformer John Calvin says, ' . . . when the Son of God put on our flesh, he also, of his own accord, experienced our human feelings, so that he did not differ in any way from his brothers, except he never sinned.'[2]

We should want to have and express emotions. To do so is only good and right, part of how God has made us. In fact, not to do so is to be less than human. We might feel and express things differently, depending on all sorts of differences between us, but we should feel – that is being Christ-like.

Right feelings

We also see that Jesus' feelings are always right and appropriate to the situation. If he feels sadness, it is because the situation is truly sad and he should respond in sadness. In fact, we can say it would have been wrong for him not to have responded that way. The same is true of joy, frustration or whatever. Jesus' emotions were always those he should have felt.

Jesus felt a whole variety of emotions: love and anger, joy and distress. We can easily assume that certain feelings, like anger, are simply wrong for Christians, but that is not the case. When faced with injustice or evil, we too should be angry, as Jesus was. Similarly, we easily assume that the mature Christian is never distressed or frustrated, but Jesus was. The challenge of course is whether we feel these things when it is right and appropriate to do so. But we should feel them.

Right degrees of feelings

Jesus' emotional response was both right – he was sad over sad things – and also to the right degree. Some things were sadder than others; some situations called for more compassion than others; some situations (like Gethsemane) were more distressing than others. Calvin says, 'Our feelings are sinful because they rush on without any restraint and know no bounds; but in Christ they were composed and regulated in obedience to God, and were completely free from sin.'[3]

Right living

We also see that Jesus lived rightly, no matter how he was feeling. So in the Garden of Gethsemane he was feeling incredible distress, but he still submitted to God's will. It was right that he felt so deeply, and it was right that he didn't back out because of his feelings. That's really important. We may feel wonderful joy and peace in God which actually helps us to live for him, but we may also feel pain, sadness and distress, and need to keep living for God within those feelings. We want to feel like Jesus did, but we also want to follow him in living for God no matter how we are feeling.

> *We want to feel like Jesus did, but we also want to follow him in living for God no matter how we are feeling.*

The challenge to feel

The first challenge for some of us may be to feel more. Some of us, because of our upbringing or Christian culture, have been taught basically to suppress emotion. That usually goes hand in hand with thinking of emotion as a bad and dangerous thing that needs to be avoided. Or at best it is seen as a neutral thing that can be ignored. But in Jesus we see that emotion is a good and a right thing.

Being unmoved and unemotional is not a Christian virtue. We must not go down the 'feelings-are-nothing' track that we touched on earlier. In being a Christian, one thing we should want to see is growth in our feelings – so that we feel more like Jesus felt. Counsellor David Powlison writes, 'God is both the angriest and the most tender person in the Bible. Jesus is both the most sorrowful and the most exultant. Are you becoming like this God and this Christ?'[4]

We see this elsewhere in Scripture. In the Psalms, people like David express their emotions: he speaks of being joyful, scared, in anguish, hopeful, awed, lonely, and so on. There's no emotional suppression going on there!

Similarly, we see this in the apostle Paul. He tells us that he is rejoicing or in anguish, depending on the situation. And it was right for him to feel that way – indeed it would have been ungodly for him not to have felt that way. Some of Paul's letters, like 2 Corinthians, are full of emotion. So we are not aiming at a detached, calm, unruffled Christianity, but at Christianity in full emotional colour.

This is a huge issue. When I studied it for the first time, I realized that I still believed that a mature Christian didn't feel very much; I had absorbed the view that Christian growth meant remaining relatively unemotional. I think that was because many of us associate being emotional with other unhealthy ideas. The emotional person is seen as unstable, fluctuating in their Christian living. We think Christian maturity means being 'steady', so we think that's the opposite of being 'emotional'.

So here's the amazing thing: in Jesus we see someone who is both steady and emotional. Someone who feels deeply, but always rightly. Someone who feels fully, but is never at the mercy of his emotions. Emotion is not the dangerous thing many of us believe. (It certainly has the potential for all sorts of dangers, and we'll come to those in due course, but those dangers don't make it a bad thing in itself.)

The challenge to feel rightly

The second area of challenge is appropriateness. We've seen Jesus' emotions as 'right', that is, appropriate. Sad situations call for sympathy; tragic situations call for compassion; good news calls for joy. So in saying we should feel rightly, I mean we should feel what is appropriate to the event or situation we are faced with.

Some people struggle with emotions being right or wrong, and I understand their concern. But we have to admit that many of our emotions are in fact wrong. I can feel joy or sadness very easily, but too often over the wrong things. I should feel joy over salvation, but instead can easily feel it because of the compliment I've just been paid. I should feel sadness over sin in my life and the world, but instead I can easily feel it because of the DIY job I've just messed up.

Of course it isn't wrong to be joyful over everyday things, whether that's my football team doing well, or passing my driving test, or whatever. But my joy over these things should also be to the right degree. Again, unfortunately, I tend to feel more joy over these sorts of things than my salvation. And it's the same with my sadness. I'm more sad over lesser things and less sad over greater things.

Here's our problem: we can feel the wrong things, or we feel right things but to wrong degrees.

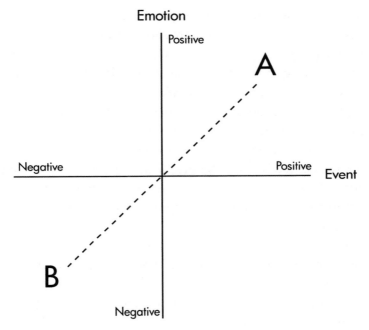

Figure 2

The graph in figure 2 shows events or situations on the horizontal axis. These may be positive events that we should be happy about or negative events that we should be sad over. The vertical axis is the emotion that these situations or events produce in us. That includes 'positive' emotions (like happiness and joy) and 'negative' emotions (like sadness or anger).

So when friends have a baby, I feel glad for them because that's a great thing – so that would be point A on the graph. When another friend loses her job, I am sad for her because that's a rubbish thing – that's point B. So first of all, I want to be in the right section of the graph. Unfortunately, I can respond with the wrong sort of emotion – feeling envious of someone's success, or secretly pleased with someone else's misfortune.

Secondly, how much should we feel, or how far up the graph should it be? How happy should I be for my friends having a baby? Compared to getting home from work early, presumably a good bit more, but compared to the forgiveness of my sins, presumably less. Similarly, with my friend losing her job, I should feel sadness for her – but the right quantity. Again, unfortunately, even when my emotion is of the right sort, I tend to feel too much or too little.

So the dotted line on the graph shows where we should want to be operating. On that line, my emotional response is appropriate in type and proportion to the event I am responding to.

You might be thinking that a graph of emotions isn't very, well, emotional. I understand this. I am fully prepared to be made fun of! And I don't mean to suggest that emotions can be reduced to a simple line. But I find such things helpful, so hopefully you will too.

So we're aiming at a fully functioning emotional life. That's how God has made us to feel. And this will need to be an emotional life where our emotions are appropriate.

We are not seeking feelings

There's another huge challenge in all of this. I'm guessing that some of you are reading this book because you struggle with your emotions and you want to feel differently. Well, I really do hope that this book will help you, but there is something we need to be clear on: we're not aiming at feeling certain things, but at being more like Christ.

What I mean is that we want to be Christ-like in feeling rightly – whatever those feelings might be. That might entail living life with a greater burden for the lost, feeling more pain over injustice or experiencing a deep sense of compassion for those around us. And I think it will also mean we feel more positive emotions like joy and peace and contentment, but the idea is not to aim at feeling certain feelings.

As I've studied this topic, that's been an issue I've needed to remind myself of. I've so easily slipped into wanting to feel a certain way – and I've justified it with reasons. And some of those reasons have been good and right. But there is a difference in perspective: do I start wanting to feel better, or to be more godly in my feelings? Do I aim at feeling something, or aim at being like Jesus?

Our aim is to have godly emotions and be more like Jesus – which will take our emotional life in many different directions.

Emotions and values

Our emotions turn on the evaluation we make of something: we make a judgment over how significant an event is, like the birth of our friends' baby or someone losing their job. We assign a certain value to that, and that value is what lies behind our emotional response. We respond much more strongly (whether positively or negatively) to those things to which we assign greater value. So if my football team is hugely important to me, then I respond with much greater emotion to its successes or failures. If I don't really care about my job, then I'm not too bothered about being offered a promotion or being shown the door.

So here's the point from our examination of Jesus' emotional responses: Jesus valued things to exactly the right degree. As a result, he always responded in the right way.

The challenge to us is to 'recalibrate' our hearts so that we too have the right values and we too express right emotions. That takes us to the topic of the next chapter: where our emotions come from.

Questions for reflection

1. Have you thought about Jesus as an example to us in his feelings before? Why or why not? What is helpful about this?
2. What strikes you from Jesus' emotional life?
3. Do you agree we are aiming at a fully functioning emotional life? Is that part of your picture of Christian maturity?
4. Which is the greater challenge for you: to feel, or to feel rightly?
5. Have you ever drifted into the danger of seeking certain feelings rather than Christ-likeness?

3
getting to the heart of emotions

We often speak of emotions as wild and unpredictable things. We think of them as a bit of a mystery that we just have to live with. Jesus however gets to the bottom of them and says that they, like so much else, flow from our hearts.

The control centre of life

We tend to use the word 'heart' today to refer to what we feel – in modern language the heart is where we locate the emotions. But in the Bible the heart isn't so much the place where we feel things: our emotional centre, but rather the place that directs our life: our control centre. It is the 'heart' of who we are!

And sometimes we use the word 'heart' in that way today, for example when we say, 'Put your heart into it' and we mean throw all of yourself into whatever it is. If I ask someone, 'What's on your heart?', I mean what is central at that precise moment.

Speaking about the heart being the control centre of life, Jesus says in Luke,

> No good tree bears bad fruit, nor does a bad tree bear good fruit. Each tree is recognized by its own fruit. People do not pick figs from thornbushes, or grapes from briers. A good man brings good things out of the good stored up in his heart, and an evil man brings evil things out of the evil stored up in his heart. For the mouth speaks what the heart is full of.
> (Luke 6:43–45)

Jesus uses the illustration of a tree and its fruit. As I write this, I can see several fruit trees outside my office. We have some apple, some damson, some cherry, and probably some others as well. But it's only just springtime, and right now you wouldn't know which tree was which sort – they're all just bare branches and twigs. But in a few months' time, you'll be able to tell easily which is which because the fruit will be hanging there in front of your eyes.

In these verses Jesus is saying that the fruit in our lives reveals what sort of 'tree' we are – it shows just what our hearts are like. What sort of fruit does he mean? He mentions the words we speak, but the picture is more general: it's our words, decisions, actions and even our emotions.

We get that general picture in the book of Proverbs:

> Above all else, guard your heart,
>   for everything you do flows from it.
> (Proverbs 4:23)

Our hearts are like the source of a spring of water, and our lives are the stream that flows from that source. Just as any bit of a river or stream that you can point to has all flowed from its spring, so *all our life flows from our hearts*. We live the lives we do, and have the emotions that we feel, because of the hearts that we have.

Our hearts' desire

This points us to the central importance of the heart. Let's look at it more carefully and think about how all of life flows from it.

In the Bible the 'heart' contains a lot of things. It is about what we think and believe; it is about what we love and hate; it is about what we hope for and what we fear. It's about our convictions, our longings and our desires. Perhaps above all, it is about what we value.

The eighteenth-century pastor and theologian Jonathan Edwards wrote a great work called *The Religious Affections*. By 'affections' Edwards meant this heart stuff that we're talking about here. He referred to it as the *inclination* of our hearts. What he meant was that we don't simply think facts about people or things; we have inclinations towards or away from them. So I don't simply think my wife is lovely; my heart is drawn to her. You don't simply think Marmite is a curious yeast extract; you either love it or hate it (as the adverts say).

We live the lives we do, and have the emotions that we feel, because of the hearts that we have.

This isn't simply bare knowledge, but my heart attitude. We might say it is what I really and truly believe about a thing or a person, as opposed to what I might think or say I believe.

Edwards says, 'True religion, in great part, consists in holy affections.'[1] His point is that a great part of real Christianity has to do with these heart attitudes rather than being solely about right knowledge and right action. Edwards was very concerned about right understanding and right living among Christians, but he said that knowledge and living must go hand in hand with right affections. So as we learn more about God, we don't simply know more. We love God more, or we are more in awe of him, or we praise him more, or display whatever attitude is appropriate to that knowledge.

This shows that there is something really important going on beneath what we think and do. I might know lots about God, but the real question is whether my heart is drawn to love and value God as result. Actually, while I might know lots of true things about God, my heart could easily be drawn to love and value other things like money, image or success.

So Edwards says that people who only have doctrine in their heads but no affection in their hearts aren't engaged in the business of real Christianity. In fact, he said that no understanding of God was worthwhile if it didn't result in greater affection for God: 'No light in the understanding is good which does not produce hot affection in the heart.'[2]

So our faith is a matter of the heart. Without right heart attitudes, we are in danger of an empty, dry and external faith.

The heart and feelings

It might seem as if we've gone a long way from the topic of emotion, and in a sense we have because we're dealing with much deeper attitudes. But it is these attitudes of the heart that lie behind our emotions. All of our life – including our feelings – flows from our hearts. All that we do is because of what we desire, love and value – the affections of our heart.

Why do I feel so quickly annoyed with my wife if she criticizes me? Is it because I think the criticism is wrong? Possibly, on occasion, although she is usually right. The real reason lies in how important my competence is to me. My heart values the idea of being competent and being seen to be competent, and criticism challenges that, so I respond strongly. My feelings flow from my heart.

Or why do we feel anxious about taking an exam? Because our hearts value the outcome. And that's not wrong. But if we are overwhelmed with anxiety, this is usually because we value it more than we should. Or we value others' opinion of our results more than we should.

Or why do I feel a lack of compassion for my Christian brother or sister going through a hard time? Is it because their suffering is not as important to me as it should be, or because I am so taken up with other things that I rate these above them and their suffering?

So (at the risk of being made fun of again), let me give you a formula for emotions (figure 3). Not that I think emotions can be reduced to a formula, but it is something I find both true and helpful. So here we go:

Figure 3

We are all faced with situations or events – what someone said or did, what job we are in, or where we live. We have a certain heart value about it: how concerned I am about that person's comment, how much I value my job, how important my house is to me. And it's the combination of the two that results in how I feel.

My job may be very important to me (high value), and suddenly I'm faced with being made redundant – so I feel very worried. On the other hand, if I don't value what I do, I don't really mind. A particular relationship might be high on my value list, and so any problems in that relationship cause me great angst, but I don't feel so worried over another relationship because my heart doesn't value it as much.

So the big issue is this: it's not so much what we feel as *why we feel it*. Emotions aren't wrong in themselves. Even 'negative' emotions like anger or frustration are often perfectly appropriate. What makes emotions wrong is when they flow from wrong heart values.

The theologian Augustine put it like this: 'We do not so much ask whether a pious soul is angry, as why he is angry; not whether he is sad, but whence comes his sadness; not whether he is afraid, but what he fears.'[3]

> *What makes emotions wrong is when they flow from wrong heart values.*

Remember we ended the last chapter saying that Jesus had right feelings, to the right degree? And the reason was because he valued everything as he should. Jesus felt rightly because he had a *good and right heart*.

The state of our hearts

The problem with our emotions then is that we have a problem with our hearts. We've been making an assumption here which we need to state out loud: *Our hearts are sinful and distorted.* Our turning against God affects every part of us. By sinning we think wrongly, act wrongly and feel wrongly. Sin throws our emotions into disorder.

In Mark 7 Jesus talks about where our sin comes from. He mentions sinful actions, but also sinful feelings like envy or greed. And he says, 'For it is from within, out of a person's heart, that evil thoughts come' (Mark 7:21).

Our problem is not fundamentally a lack of knowledge or willpower but a wrong orientation of the heart. So the Puritan writer Thomas Boston says of a person in our sinful state,

> He loves what he should hate and hates what he should love;
> rejoices in what he ought to mourn for, and mourns for what he
> should rejoice in; glories in his shame, and is ashamed of his glory;
> abhors what he should desire, and desires what he should abhor.[4]

We love the wrong things, and even when we love the right things, we love them too much or too little.

John Calvin compares our emotions to those of Jesus, when he says, 'In short, if you compare his passions with ours, they will differ not less than pure and clear water, flowing in a gentle course, differs from dirty and muddy foam.'[5] It's a really key moment in dealing with our emotions when we take this point on board. Do *you* accept that your emotions are like dirty, muddy water, compared to the crystal clear stream of Jesus' feelings? We need to accept that our hearts are rotten, and therefore produce rotten feelings – that's our starting point.

But thankfully it's not our finishing point. First, we are forgiven for such rotten feelings – Jesus paid the price for them, and so we can confess them to God and be forgiven. We are forgiven for sinful feelings just as much as for sinful actions. More than that, we are clothed in the righteousness of Christ, including his righteous feelings. So we can know forgiveness and we can stand confident before God in Christ. That's a good start!

But more than that, God is in the business of renewing our hearts. He cleanses them by his Spirit. Paul writes,

> But when the kindness and love of God our Saviour appeared,
> he saved us, not because of righteous things we had done, but

because of his mercy. He saved us through the washing of
rebirth and renewal by the Holy Spirit, whom he poured out
on us generously through Jesus Christ our Saviour.
(Titus 3:4–6)

That 'washing and renewal' of the Spirit cleans up the rubbish
dump of our hearts so that we love and desire the right things.
We will start to hate sin and love holiness. We will feel compassion, contentment, joy, peace, fear and every other emotion.
And we will do so because our hearts will start to value things
rightly.

But I used the word 'start'. And I did so deliberately because
that cleansing of our hearts doesn't completely wash them
out. Rather it is the start of a heart 'clean-up' that will continue
throughout our lives.

So we see two things. First, our aim of a good and right
emotional life is part of God's process of making us more
like Christ. Feeling rightly is
part of God's work in us, part
of Christian growth, and that's
significant because we can easily
think of feelings as pretty low
down the priority list with God.
Working on our emotional life
isn't a luxury or an indulgence,
but part of becoming more like
Jesus.

> *Working on our
> emotional life isn't
> a luxury or
> an indulgence,
> but part of
> becoming more
> like Jesus.*

Secondly, we're seeing that
this process focuses on our
hearts. We feel what we feel because of the hearts we have.
Our emotions come from what we love, what we desire, what
we value. In order to grow, we are going to have to do some
work on our hearts.

It's all about love (and hate)

We can see this point more clearly by thinking about specific feelings. Feelings flow ultimately from what we love, and what we hate.

My daughter had had a teddy bear from when she was born. She loved that bear dearly. When she had it, she felt happy and content. On one occasion when she lost it, she felt sad and cried. But when she found it again a day later, she felt joyful. On another occasion, when we didn't know where it was, she felt anxious and concerned. And as it became clear that we might have left it somewhere while on holiday, she became upset. And when we broke the news that there was no way we could go back for it, she cried (but in the end got over it pretty quickly).

Do you see that, with something you love, you feel different emotions depending on different circumstances? If you don't have it, you feel a desire or a longing for it; if you think you'll get it soon, then there's expectation and excitement; and if someone gives it to you, you feel gratitude, and so on.

Or you can turn this around with something that we hate. If we face something we hate (like an illness), we feel fear or anxiety. If we escape it, we feel relief. If we know we can't escape it, we feel depressed.

The same thing works for our feelings towards other people. If we love and value someone, then we will feel pleased for them when something good happens, or compassionate towards them when something bad happens.

Paul's story

My career was going so well. I'd shown some initiative and had been rewarded for it. I was climbing the ladder faster than those around me. It was great. And I gave myself to it with all my heart. All this gave me great satisfaction and a feeling of confidence. Until the day I fell ill.

I've not been able to work properly since then, and I've felt devastated, and then depressed. Of course being ill long term is rubbish, but there's been more than that behind my feelings of devastation and depression.

I just loved being successful. I loved being *seen* to be successful. I loved it more than anything else in life. When that was there, I felt great. When it was taken away, I felt terrible. It's shown me what I really loved.

All our feelings flow from what our hearts love. Augustine said, 'The feelings are bad if the love is bad, and good if the love is good.'[6] As we saw earlier, we feel wrongly because we love the wrong things, and we love the right things too much or too little.

The big question then is: what do we love?

The Bible tells us that we can love ourselves, money, an image, pleasure and loads of other things. And this will result in all kinds of feelings. Growth as a Christian then means growth in loving rightly, or having the right heart values. Becoming more Christ-like in our emotions flows from growth in a right heart.

Examples of a right heart

We see this in the example of the apostle Paul. In the letter to the Philippians he tells us he is rejoicing. But when he's writing, he's sitting in a Roman prison – not a rejoicing kind of place! So why is he full of joy? 'In all my prayers for all of you, I always pray with joy because of your partnership in the gospel from the first day until now' (Philippians 1:4–5). The Philippians have supported Paul's mission work, and that means that, as he thinks of them and prays for them in his prison cell, a smile comes to his face – he prays with joy.

Why?

Because he values their partnership in the gospel. He loves to see it, and so he rejoices in it.

Secondly, he says that being in prison has served to 'advance the gospel' (1:12). That's because people have grown in confidence and are spreading the gospel. Unfortunately some people are spreading the gospel from wrong motives, thinking they can stir up trouble for Paul. But says Paul in conclusion, 'But what does it matter? The important thing is that in every way, whether from false motives or true, Christ is preached. And because of this I rejoice' (Philippians 1:18).

So despite prison and people trying to stir up trouble, Paul is rejoicing.

Why?

Because he values the spread of the gospel. He loves to see it, and so he rejoices in it.

I'm not saying that Paul was happy about his cell, or that he pretended that life was great. But I am saying that Paul's heart values showed themselves in joy.

Jan's story

I attended a church weekend away at a conference centre in a beautiful part of Scotland. A couple of walkers stopped me to ask if there was anywhere they could have lunch. So I invited them to lunch in the conference centre. It turned out that they were from the same part of the world as me, and we chatted away about home. As the conversation went on, I was able to talk to them about the weekend, the church and the gospel.

> There was no great outcome, but I think it made them think. I had a real sense of God organizing things and of me being used by God. Evangelism is so important, and I don't get many opportunities like that to share the gospel. I felt so happy that afternoon.

Elsewhere we see Paul in anguish over other Christians – because he's not sure if they're holding on to the true gospel (Galatians 4:19–20). Or we see him anxious over the health of a colleague (Philippians 2:27–28). All these feelings flow from what Paul loved.

We see this too in biblical commands for us to rejoice when facing trials. James tells us,

> Consider it pure joy, my brothers and sisters, whenever you face trials of many kinds, because you know that the testing of your faith produces perseverance. Let perseverance finish its work so that you may be mature and complete, not lacking anything. (James 1:2–4)

The Christian isn't to rejoice in trials because they are good things, but because of what the trials will achieve – perseverance and eventually maturity. But to rejoice in trials, I have to value maturity more than my comforts. I will rejoice in trials if I have the right values and my heart loves the right things.

So the mature Christian will love the right things. And that love will result in all kinds of right feelings. The mature Christian will:

- love what is good (Titus 1:8)
- delight in God's law (Psalm 119:16)
- feel grateful for salvation (Colossians 2:7)

- desire to please God in all things (2 Corinthians 5:9)
- rejoice in the unity of the church (Philippians 2:2)
- be jealous for God's glory (2 Corinthians 11:2)
- rejoice to see the gospel spread (Philippians 1:18)
- hate what is evil (Romans 12:9)
- mourn over sin (James 4:9)
- be anxious over a stumbling Christian (Galatians 4:19–20)
- have concern for the welfare of the church (Philippians 2:20)
- weep for those who refuse the gospel (Romans 9:2–4)
- feel compassion for those suffering (Hebrews 13:3)
- long for the new creation (2 Peter 3:13)

And more!

A window on the heart

This view of emotions has a really helpful practical outcome. It means that our emotions can be used as windows into what is happening in our hearts. I don't mean that that's their primary function – far from it. But they do give us an insight into what we really love.

So if I feel annoyed, I can ask the question, 'Why do I feel annoyed?' And I can find an answer deeper than simply: 'Because that person was rude to me.' A little reflection results in me saying, 'Because that person was rude to me, and so they offended my sense of importance, and they did so in front of my girlfriend.' I got as annoyed as I did because of how much I value my importance, and how much I value the approval of my girlfriend.

Of course in some situations it might be that I can see why I am annoyed – and that my annoyance is entirely appropriate. However, often it isn't, and asking the question shows me how it flows from my heart.

Rather than emotions being wild and unpredictable, there is actually a reason for them. It's not always an obvious reason – and it can sometimes be hard to work it out – but it is a reason that flows from my heart. We sometimes think emotions are irrational things, but that is not the case. People are irrational and have irrational emotions, but there's nothing irrational about emotions themselves.

That is significant because it provides a way into changing our emotions. As we said in the last chapter, what we want is to have appropriate and proportional emotions – right emotions to the right extent. To get there, I need to know where my emotions are coming from. I need to know, for example, that my annoyance comes from my love of my competence. That means I go to work on my heart on how much I love my competence. That's where the work will need to take place so that my feelings can change.

> Brian's reflection
>
> I can easily feel self-pity. Someone might snub me, or I might fail at something like an exam, or I might be treated unfairly, and then I will feel so sorry for myself. I feel like everyone should notice me and pander to me!
>
> As I've reflected, I've realized something of where that self-pity is coming from. I think too highly of myself, which means that any slight against my character is really serious to me. It flows too from my insecurity. I want to perform well so that I can think well of myself. That means that any failure or lack of achievement threatens me. It's increased too by thinking the worst of other people. I interpret people's actions and comments in the worst possible light and want to see myself as the innocent victim.

I've realized I need to:

- consider my limitations and my failures and so be humble;
- remember that I too do and say things that can hurt;
- think more highly of others than of myself;
- not presume the worst of other people's motivations;
- remind myself that I am accepted by God's grace despite my failures.

A word of warning! What I am encouraging is greater emotional awareness – why I feel what I feel. We want that awareness so that we can see what we love and value in our hearts, so that we can change. What I am not encouraging however is endless introspection. This depends a bit on your personality. Some people never ask themselves why they feel something; they're too busy pressing on with what they think they should be doing next. I want to encourage them to reflect and use their emotions as a window into their hearts. Others however are always asking themselves why they feel something already. I don't want them to take their emotional temperature every hour!

Contributory factors

This focus on the heart isn't to deny the fact that many other factors feed into how we feel. Indeed, one thing that makes emotions so complicated is that so many different factors shape them. Here are some of the most important ones.

Personality

We say that one person is a little dour, whereas someone else is always chirpy. One person might cry quite easily at something, whereas someone else is relatively unmoved by the same thing. This is all a function of our different personalities. God has made us as different people and that is something to rejoice in.

Background and upbringing

Our background exerts a huge influence on us. And how our parents expressed themselves emotionally has a strong shaping influence. Some will have been brought up having being shown affection (or anger) in very obvious ways. Others will have received little demonstration of feelings. There is also variation in how we will have been encouraged or discouraged to express our feelings. Some will have been told 'not to be such a cry-baby', whereas others will have been encouraged 'to let it all out'.

Culture

We might speak disparagingly of another culture as being 'emotional' (maybe the Spanish), or another as being 'cold' (maybe the Norwegians). Of course when we do so, we are using ourselves as the reference point! Which shows that how we expect to feel and express emotions is a very cultural business. And within a country there will be subcultures: a stiff public-school-type culture is going to express emotion very differently from a council-estate culture.

Memories

Our memories are also very significant in how we respond emotionally. If hearing of a death reminds someone of their personal bereavement, they will probably respond with far greater emotion than someone who hasn't experienced death up close. And it doesn't have to be as obvious as that. Distant unpleasant memories of anger at home can mean that we feel fearful when we hear raised voices, even if we don't make the association ourselves.

Tiredness, health and hormones

We are physical beings, and our physical state affects how we feel. I know when I'm getting tired because I cry much more easily. But tiredness for other people means that they start to feel emotionally numb. Poor health can have similar effects. And many will testify to variations in hormonal levels playing havoc with their emotions.

We mustn't discount any of these factors. However, we must also recognize that they are not the actual source of our emotions. One way to think about them is this: they have a magnifying or minimizing effect on what I feel. They might increase it – so what would have made me a little irritated now sends me screaming up the wall. They might reduce it, so that what would have had me feeling sorry for someone is shrunk to a brief pitying thought. I can feel less or more depending on these issues, but they do not actually cause me to feel in the first place.

In practice this means we mustn't discount these factors. It means for example that if we feel flat and despondent, we should ask whether we are eating and sleeping well. It means that, if we know we're tired or hormonal, we don't pay more attention to our high levels of emotion than we should. It means that we will expect differences between us that are not wrong or right, but just differences. It means we don't judge one another and don't feel guilty or superior ourselves.

But we don't stop taking responsibility for how we feel. That all started in our hearts.

Questions and ideas for reflection

1. What is so important about the Bible's picture of our hearts as the control centre of life?
2. What do you make of the formula for where emotions come from?
3. Do you agree with Calvin's comment that our emotions are like 'dirty and muddy foam' compared to Jesus?
4. Why do our emotions come from what we love?
5. Think of some examples of feelings you've experienced recently, and trace the connection back to what you love.
6. What's helpful about emotions being 'windows on our hearts'?

4
how to get emotional

How do we get this fully functioning emotional life that I described earlier? How do we become more like Christ in our emotional life? We know that any change will come from our hearts, but how?

Do nothing: emotions are expected

My first point is that we don't necessarily have to do anything! Emotion is simply expected in the lives of God's people as a natural response. That response might be to God, to all that he is and all that he has done; it might be a response to our sinfulness, or to something else. But whatever it is, emotion is part of the normal life of the Christian.

Paul says to the Colossian Christians, 'So then, just as you received Christ Jesus as Lord, continue to live your lives in him, rooted and built up in him, strengthened in the faith as you were taught, and overflowing with thankfulness' (Colossians 2:6–7). He is describing the normal, ongoing

Christian life of growth in Jesus. But notice that part of that normal Christian life is 'thankfulness'. This is one of those heart attitudes we saw earlier. It is deeper than a feeling, but it does involve my feelings. Overflowing with thankfulness means feeling gratitude in my heart. And this is simply expected; in fact Paul sets the bar very high – we're to be 'overflowing' with thankfulness.

We see something similar in the Psalms when David reflects on God's goodness and love to him. Here's an example:

> Praise be to the LORD,
>   for he has heard my cry for mercy.
> The LORD is my strength and my shield;
>   my heart trusts in him, and he helps me.
> My heart leaps for joy,
>   and with my song I praise him.
> (Psalm 28:6–7)

David calls on God for help. God responds to David and saves him. And the result is that David cries out in praise to God. See that his heart 'leaps for joy'. This is a natural response.

I remember one occasion when our car broke down. We were on the motorway a long way from home late in the evening. The car refused to start. And we had no breakdown insurance. I really started to worry and wonder what to do. And then a breakdown truck pulled up behind us on the hard shoulder. I didn't have to tell myself to be happy – my heart leapt with joy! I was so relieved and desperately grateful.

That's how David feels. He's so thankful that he breaks out into song. In the light of God's goodness to us, it's natural to feel such things.

Chris's story

I'd been away from home on a trip and had been reflecting on life. God had been bringing various things to mind. One of the biggest was my pride. I'd started to see just how proud I was – it was ugly and uncomfortable. And then I went to a Christian conference. During one of the sessions we were singing about God's ongoing love and forgiveness. It struck me – he loves me still, and he keeps forgiving this horrible pride of mine. And as I reflected on this, I was almost overwhelmed with feelings of gratitude, and as I sang the tears flowed down my cheeks.

But these expected feelings are not limited to feelings of joy and thankfulness. For example, speaking about God's laws, David says,

> They are more precious than gold,
> > than much pure gold;
> they are sweeter than honey,
> > than honey from the honeycomb.
> (Psalm 19:10)

Do you see his attitude? He doesn't simply believe that God's law is true and right; he doesn't simply want to obey it and give himself to following it, but he feels something about it!

Again, in Psalm 119, the psalmist speaks about obeying God's law:

> I rejoice in following your statutes
> > as one rejoices in great riches.
> (Psalm 119:14)

The psalmist rejoices to live by God's rules. Just like people would rejoice at winning the lottery, he rejoices in obeying God.

Or we see people feeling sad over sin in the book of Ezra. This comes at a point where God's people realize just how badly they have disobeyed God, and they are struck by their sin. Here is how it's described: 'While Ezra was praying and confessing, weeping and throwing himself down before the house of God, a large crowd of Israelites – men, women and children – gathered around him. They too wept bitterly' (Ezra 10:1).

This isn't just saying, 'I'm a sinner'; this is being convicted and struck to the heart. It shows itself in bitter tears. And there's no sense that this is whipped up; people have come to see how awful their sin is, and the natural response is that they feel really terrible.

Sarah's story

Most of the time I don't really think about my sin. I know it's there, but I don't feel anything about it. But there was a time recently when I remembered a moment from years ago. It was an attitude to my sister, where I didn't want her to be successful, or at least I wanted to be more successful than her. In fact it was worse than that – I actually felt happy that life had gone pear-shaped for her, because then I would be more of a success by comparison.

This reminded me of looking back at an old photograph and seeing yourself looking different. Normally that means seeing how bad your hairstyle or dress was. But here it was seeing how horrible my heart could be, and I felt terrible.

So emotions are expected as a natural and normal part of the Christian life. When people see what God has done, this results in feelings of joy and thankfulness. Or when people consider the goodness of his Word, they love it, or when people see their sin clearly, they mourn over it. There is no sense in these passages that emotions need to be worked on. They were what was appropriate and what flowed out naturally.

God has renewed our hearts by his Spirit so that we start to feel rightly. We do, at least to some extent, mourn our sin and value our salvation. And so we do to some extent feel rightly over these things.

So at least let's be encouraged that we're not starting from completely the wrong position. Many good and right emotions will flow naturally from us, and we should thank God for those right feelings that we have already.

Recalibrate your heart: emotions are commanded

As well as emotions being expected as natural, they are also commanded. This is vital to grasp because it means that we can take responsibility for how we feel; we can and should influence our emotions.

We need to think about this carefully though. I clearly can't simply command myself to feel thankful or joyful or loving or anything else. Saying, 'Graham, feel happy!' doesn't achieve very much. We can't control our emotions like we control the direction of a car, steering it wherever we want. In fact 'control' isn't really the right verb. Let's look at some of the commands and then think what we should call it.

Joy in salvation

Jesus sends his disciples out on a preaching and healing tour. Here's what happens when they come back:

The seventy-two returned with joy and said, 'Lord, even the
demons submit to us in your name.'

He replied, 'I saw Satan fall like lightning from heaven.
I have given you authority to trample on snakes and
scorpions and to overcome all the power of the enemy;
nothing will harm you. However, do not rejoice that the
spirits submit to you, but rejoice that your names are written
in heaven.'
(Luke 10:17–20)

The disciples come back from their tour rejoicing in their
new-found abilities – that the demons submit to them. But
Jesus tells them not to rejoice in that, but in the fact of their
salvation instead.

Jesus is saying, don't rejoice in X, rejoice in Y instead. That's
huge! This means we must be able to tell ourselves to rejoice
in one thing more than another; we must be able to direct our
emotions – in this case what we rejoice in.

The disciples were rejoicing in the spirits submitting to
them because they thought that was a great thing. We too
rejoice in what we think is good and valuable. What Jesus is
telling the disciples to do is to rate their salvation as better and
more valuable! He's telling them to recalibrate their hearts,
so that they value their salvation more highly than the gifts
he has given them.

So we can be commanded to rejoice in our salvation more
than we rejoice in other things – even good things. We can
recalibrate our hearts to love our salvation more than anything else.

This is a bit like children and presents. Sometimes my
children open a present and they are desperately disappointed
– you can see it in their face. And the grandparents aren't
too impressed with a child who pulls off the wrapping paper

and then starts crying! But sometimes it's because the child doesn't understand what the present is. And so I explain something about what it is, how it works, or why they'll enjoy it. And a minute later they're smiling and saying, 'Thank you!'

What's changed? They now appreciate how valuable the present is. And the more they appreciate it, the more they rejoice in it. So Jesus can command us to rejoice in our salvation – which is telling us to appreciate that salvation for what it really is, to change what our hearts value and love most.

Mourning over sin

We're not only commanded to rejoice though. Here's James telling people to feel bad over their sin: 'Wash your hands, you sinners, and purify your hearts, you double-minded. Grieve, mourn and wail. Change your laughter to mourning and your joy to gloom' (James 4:8–9).

Now James only writes this because he knows something about his readers – that they are double-minded sinners! Christians aren't to walk around always feeling awful on account of their sin, because our sin is forgiven (that's why we feel joyful!). But when we are struck by our sin, or when we realize that we are resisting God in some way, then we should do as James says – grieve, mourn and wail.

We saw earlier that this can happen naturally when we see our sin clearly. But James is dealing with a situation where that's not happening – the people aren't feeling as they should do about sin. James doesn't want them just to pretend to be sad when they don't see what they're doing wrong – that would be fake grief. He's trying to get them to see how bad their sin is, how awful and ugly their attitude is, and to see how they should respond and feel.

Loving God

Here's Moses speaking in Deuteronomy: 'Love the LORD your God with all your heart and with all your soul and with all your strength' (Deuteronomy 6:5).

We are commanded to love God with all that we are. We can really struggle with this command because of all the ideas surrounding 'love' today. We speak about falling in and out of love, which makes it sound like we have no control over it – it just happens.

That makes commanding us to love seem weird. But love in the Bible isn't an emotion we happen to end up feeling; it is a decision we take to focus our affections and loyalty. Loving God is a decision to set our hearts on him, value him and so live for him. But that doesn't mean it's emptied of feeling. It's a decision to value God, which involves feeling a certain way towards him.

And this command has reasons attached: Moses has spoken about all that God has done for the people in rescuing them from Egypt. He also speaks about God's uniqueness and God's commitment in loving them. So the command to love God flows from who God is and what he has done for us.

Of course I might see those things about God and naturally respond in love to him. But we are also commanded, which shows we can direct our hearts in what we love.

It's a bit like marriage. Sometimes I simply love my wife without thinking about it – I enjoy spending time with her, enjoy who she is, and I respond in love. But I am also commanded to love her. I can't create a certain feeling in my heart, but I can focus my heart on her, reminding myself about her and valuing her.

It's the same with our love for God. We can't simply make ourselves feel love for him, but we can direct our hearts to him and value him for all that he is and has done for us.

Not worrying

Jesus speaks about the security we can have, and commands us not to worry:

> Therefore I tell you, do not worry about your life, what you will eat or drink; or about your body, what you will wear. Is not life more than food, and the body more than clothes? Look at the birds of the air; they do not sow or reap or store away in barns, and yet your heavenly Father feeds them. Are you not much more valuable than they?
>
> (Matthew 6:25–26)

We do so easily worry though! And to obey Jesus' command we need to remind ourselves of the truth of his words about God's care and concern for us. If I really believe those things – if my heart trusts them – then I will be at peace.

Sometimes I am aware of God's sovereign care and concern for me, and I experience peace as a result. At other times though I need to be told not to worry. Which is the same as being told to remember those truths and apply them to myself in whatever anxiety-provoking situation I find myself in.

Let's sum up

This is a significant step forward! Do you see that the same emotions are both commanded and expected? So a right emotion might be there automatically, but when it's not, we are told to have it. That means that, while we can feel what is right and appropriate, we don't always do so, but we can do something about it.

This is where we need to go back to understanding the 'fall', when we turned away from God (Genesis 3). We were made as thinking, feeling, acting people, and at first our thinking, feeling and acting were good and perfect. Adam and

Eve thought right thoughts, felt right feelings and acted rightly! But with our rebellion against God, every area of life was affected. We think wrongly, act wrongly – and we feel wrongly. Some people might feel hesitant about saying that any feelings are 'wrong'. I understand this concern because feelings are so complicated. But we must see that feelings can indeed be sinful.

That's what lies behind these commands to feel a certain way. We need to be told and directed. And the good news is that we can take some responsibility for how we feel. That must be true or these commands are meaningless. We saw above that we can't really speak of controlling our emotions – they are just not that controllable! But we've seen also that we can focus our thinking and change what our hearts value. All these commands are to understand something, see something, realize something, respond to something, value something – and our feelings flow from that.

Our feelings flow from our hearts, and so these commands are commands to recalibrate our hearts and value things rightly.

Our feelings flow from our hearts, and so these commands are *commands to recalibrate our hearts and value things rightly*.

We've seen:

- joy because I value salvation above all else;
- sorrow over sin because I see it is so wrong;
- love for God because he is more important to me than anything else;
- peace because I trust God's love and provision.

We could add more. But for now see the principle at work: for each of these we are commanded to have right thinking and therefore right feelings. And so for each we need to speak truth to our hearts about what is more important or valuable, or what is true or false.

We can't turn our feelings on and off at will, but we can influence them. It's worth knowing that in years gone by this was how people thought about emotions, seeing them as part of the will, which they could direct. There was a change a couple of hundred years ago where people started to speak of emotions as things that simply happened. Alongside that, they started to think of them as things we weren't responsible for. We've inherited that thinking, which is why today we so easily think we can't do anything about how we feel. That's really unhelpful. The older picture is the more biblical one – directing our hearts as to what they love and value, and so directing our emotions.

Pray: emotions are to be asked for

Emotions are also to be asked for. Here is part of Paul's prayer for the Colossian Christians: ' . . . being strengthened with all power according to his glorious might so that you may have great endurance and patience, and giving joyful thanks to the Father, who has qualified you to share in the inheritance of his holy people in the kingdom of light' (Colossians 1:11–12). Paul longs that they will be filled with joyful thanks over what God has done. Thanksgiving is to be expected, and elsewhere such thankfulness is commanded, but that doesn't stop Paul praying for it.

We see something similar in a prayer in Romans: 'May the God of hope fill you with all joy and peace as you trust in him, so that you may overflow with hope by the power of the Holy Spirit' (Romans 15:13). Here Paul prays that the people will be filled with two emotions: joy and peace, with the result that they overflow with another: hope. Notice that this work of God only happens as they 'trust in him'. They don't just sit back and get filled! Rather Paul sees them trusting God's promises and goodness, and being filled by God as they do that. But in the end, they will overflow with hope by the power of the Holy Spirit.

Another example is of Paul asking that God will fill Christians with love for one another: 'May the Lord make your love increase and overflow for each other and for everyone else, just as ours does for you' (1 Thessalonians 3:12). Elsewhere, love between Christians is simply expected or commanded, but here it is prayed for. God is the one who will make their love increase and overflow.

We can see the same thing from another angle. Think of the fruit of the Spirit in Galatians 5: 'But the fruit of the Spirit is love, joy, peace, forbearance, kindness, goodness, faithfulness, gentleness and self-control' (Galatians 5:22–23). This is more of a character description – or heart attitudes. But most of these attitudes involve an emotional element. And the point is that this is something the Spirit will produce in us. Again this doesn't mean that we sit back and the fruit just appears. Paul says in the same passage that we are to walk or live by the Spirit and keep in step with the Spirit. So we are to be active in this work of 'fruit production', but ultimately it is something that God gives us.

The same feelings that are expected and commanded are also to be asked for. This means that good and right emotions are part of God's work in us. God is working in his people by his Spirit, to re-fashion them, to make them more like Christ, more as they were designed to be. He is making us more human. And that work of remaking us includes remaking how we feel.

And so we must pray that God would be at work, giving us right feelings. If Paul prayed for thankfulness, peace and joy in Christians' lives, so should we. Christian growth is only done by the Spirit's work in us, so we should constantly be asking him to be at work. If we think we can change our emotions by ourselves, we are sadly mistaken.

So pray that God would give you godly feelings: joy in salvation, love for him, peace in his sovereign care, concern for fellow Christians, compassion for the lost, and more, much more.

Pray for these things for yourself, for others, and for your church.

Of course we could easily become unbalanced here so that our prayer life orientates around us feeling good. That could mean we keep asking God for things so we simply feel nice feelings. We're not aiming at feeling certain feelings; we're aiming at a godly life that includes our feelings. Pray that God would be working on that in you by his Spirit.

So how will we get the right and appropriate emotional life that is like Jesus?

Partly through a natural response to God and his truth. As we consider salvation, we'll feel joy; as we consider sin, we'll feel sorrow; as we consider the new creation, we'll feel hope. And so on. We should want and expect there to be an emotional component in our response to God and his wonderful gospel.

The right emotional life will come as we follow God's commands and recalibrate our hearts. We are to give ourselves to right responses, including our emotions. So we look to repent of our wrong beliefs and values, and retune our hearts. And we hope to see the right feelings flow and the wrong feelings halted as a result.

The right emotional life will come ultimately as God works in us by his Spirit. So we should pray that God will be at work in us, giving us right hearts that believe the truth and value right things. We should pray that God will bring a hatred of sin and evil, a love of what is good and right, and that he will fill us with love, joy, peace and hope.

Questions and ideas for reflection

1. What good and godly emotions have you found occurring 'automatically' in your life as a Christian?
2. What do you think of the idea of emotions being commanded?
3. Try to identify an area where you want to change your heart values and so feel differently.
4. Do you pray for godly emotions? Why or why not?
5. What do you find encouraging from this chapter?
6. What do you find challenging from this chapter?
7. What questions have been raised about emotions?

5
putting emotions in their right place

We've seen that:

- emotions are a significant part of the Christian life;
- Jesus gives us the perfect model of feeling fully and feeling rightly;
- emotions flow from our hearts and what we love;
- emotions are expected, commanded and to be prayed for.

In the second half of this book we're going to look at emotions in practice. But before that, let's see the wider framework for our emotions.

Thinking, feeling and acting

We need to spend a moment connecting our feelings with our thinking and our acting. Let's start by looking at Psalm 97:

The LORD reigns, let the earth be glad;
    let the distant shores rejoice.
Clouds and thick darkness surround him;
    righteousness and justice are the foundation of his throne.
Fire goes before him
    and consumes his foes on every side.
His lightning lights up the world;
    the earth sees and trembles.
The mountains melt like wax before the LORD,
    before the Lord of all the earth.
The heavens proclaim his righteousness,
    and all peoples see his glory.

All who worship images are put to shame,
    those who boast in idols –
    worship him, all you gods!
(Psalm 97:1–7)

What an amazing image of God! He's pictured like a thunderstorm with dark clouds and lightning – a heart-stopping sight. So heart-stopping that the earth trembles before him, and the mountains melt. This is a picture of God's awesome power and might. No wonder there's a reminder that anyone who worships idols instead of this real true God will be ashamed. This is the true God whom everyone should worship.

It goes on:

Zion hears and rejoices
    and the villages of Judah are glad
    because of your judgments, LORD.
For you, LORD, are the Most High over all the earth;
    you are exalted far above all gods.
(Psalm 97:8–9)

The focus moves from God to God's people. See what happens: 'Zion hears . . . ' God's people hear these truths about God and how do they respond? They rejoice. They are glad that their God is like this – the one who is exalted above all other gods. Those truths bring joy and gladness to them.

The psalm ends with these words:

Let those who love the LORD hate evil,
for he guards the lives of his faithful ones
and delivers them from the hand of the wicked.
Light shines on the righteous
and joy on the upright in heart.
Rejoice in the LORD, you who are righteous,
and praise his holy name.
(Psalm 97:10–12)

The focus is still on God's people, but now it moves to how they should live. Those who love the Lord are called to live differently – to hate evil. They are called to live under the protection of their God, trusting him as the one who will guard and deliver them. Finally they are called to rejoice in him and praise him.

Why have we looked at this psalm? Simply because it is a classic example of thinking, feeling and acting all joined together in Scripture. I could have chosen many other passages to illustrate this – this isn't unusual; this is normal.

Truth about God leads us to feelings towards God and actions in living for him. That's the standard biblical pattern: truth is proclaimed, truth is heard, understood and believed, and feelings and actions flow out as a result.

When I was a student, I was told an illustration of where emotions fit into the Christian life. It involved a picture of a train of three parts: the engine representing facts, the next carriage representing faith, and the guard wagon at the end representing feelings. The point was that we should put our faith in the facts, and then our feelings would follow on behind.

That illustration can be told in a way that would make you think that feelings weren't very important, and you should basically forget about them. I have been arguing that that's not the case at all in the Christian life. But the illustration does have something helpful to it, and it is this ordering of our response to God. God reveals himself to us through his Word, the Bible. That's where we find out what he is like, what he has done, what he has promised, and so on. And our first step is to understand and to respond to this truth. So there is a priority of the truth of the Word. Important as feelings may be, they are secondary to the truth of the Word – they flow from that truth.

This means that feelings are not to be used to judge what is right or wrong, not to be used as a guide to life, not to tell us truth about God and ourselves, not to be treated as indicators of how God feels about us. *We must not put feelings above the place of the Word.*

I'm not undermining all that I have said so far about the importance of feelings. I am simply saying they must be in their right place. And the right place is as part of our response to God's truth. And they are not the only response – there is also action. Feeling deeply about God, but not living for him, isn't right either.

The place of the mind
So in all our discussion on the place of feelings we mustn't lose the place of the mind. In fact, if we get our priorities right, we should rate the mind as even more important.

We often divide people into 'intellectual' and 'emotional' types. Take Lee who is a classic intellectual. He's only worried about what to think and believe; he spends loads of time debating, reading and thinking about ideas. He obsesses about whether something is right or wrong. He's frustrated that other people don't seem so worried about whether a point in a Bible study or sermon is correct.

Compare Lee to Mike. Mike feels deeply. He is always reflecting on how he feels and can't help talking about it. He is either really up or really down – never just level. He makes decisions based on how he feels, whether they seem very logical or not. He's frustrated that other people seem cold towards God, and don't join in when he enthuses about what he felt in a time of worship.

Mike and Lee are stereotypes. And we've got to say that both are unhealthy! What we want is a connection between our thinking and our feeling. As in the psalm, our feelings should flow from truth.

That means there's nothing good, healthy or godly about feeling in itself. There's nothing necessarily right about deep experiences. Lots of religions claim those, and lots of non-Christians feel deeply. The question isn't whether I feel very much; the question is whether I feel rightly. And to feel rightly, I must have feelings that flow from truth.

This also means there is nothing good, healthy or godly about lots of knowledge in itself. There's nothing necessarily helpful about knowing lots of facts and having a very deep understanding of theology. Lots of unbelievers understand Christian theology. In fact even the demons have good theological knowledge (see James 2:19). The question isn't whether I know lots; the question is how I respond to what I know. Right knowledge must flow into right feeling and living.

But this also means we should be really positive about the place of the mind in the Christian life. Good feelings flow from good understanding. So the better I understand something, the more I should feel about it. Deep thoughts about God should lead to deep feelings for God, clear understanding of God to a warm heart.

The Puritan Thomas Goodwin wrote this: 'Thoughts and affections are the mutual causes of each other . . . Thoughts are the bellows that kindle and inflame affections; and then if they are inflamed, they cause thoughts to boil.'[1] Goodwin is saying that our thinking about God leads to warm hearts, but more than that, if our hearts are warm towards God, we think more about him. Think of someone who's fallen in love. As they think about their loved one, they feel love for them, and as they feel love for them, they keep thinking about them.

Knowledge and affection should go hand in hand. So we've got to stop dividing thinking and feeling. Think of the stereotypes we started with. Lee should never be happy simply to understand something or come to a conclusion that something is right. He should push himself to ask how he should feel and live in the light of that truth. He should want to be more in awe of God, more amazed at God, more thankful to God. That doesn't mean Lee is negative about learning – no, he's even more positive about it because it leads to a whole-person response to God.

Mike should want his feelings to be based on truth. He should seek a secure foundation for his emotions, and work at living on that foundation, rather than being swayed by whatever he happens to feel. He should want to come to clear convictions based on Scripture, and have feelings in the light of them. That doesn't mean that Mike should be negative about feelings – no, he can be even more positive about them, because they are based on truth about God.

The place of the will

There's another issue for Mike and Lee though – and that is that understanding and feeling must also be joined with action.

So let's introduce a third stereotype. (I'm going to make all these people blokes just so that no-one can accuse me of saying men or women are more prone to one stereotype than another!) Tim is focused on living for God. He gives himself to serving in church – he helps lead the youth group and does the PA on Sunday mornings. He's also a rep for a Christian charity caring for homeless people, and he volunteers at the charity's hostel in town. He's also involved in a child-sponsorship scheme in majority-world countries. Tim is frustrated with other Christians who aren't as keen on these sorts of activities as he is.

As we saw in Psalm 97, truth about God and feelings towards God should lead to living for God. But the challenge for Tim is his motivation for what he's doing. Does all his activity flow from truth about God, and does he do it feeling something for God? Back in the psalm it was 'those who love the Lord' who lived differently. And they loved the Lord because of the truth about him.

There is nothing good or godly about lots of activity in itself. There's nothing necessarily right about serving people or living a moral life. Lots of other religions serve people; lots of non-Christians have high moral standards. The question isn't how much I do, but whether my life flows from right knowledge about God and right feeling towards him.

So Tim should remind himself of the importance of knowledge and feeling. He should want to grow in his understanding of God and his attitude to God, seeing these as a foundation for his service. As he works, he should remind himself that he is doing all he does because he is someone who 'loves the Lord'. That will actually mean there is greater motivation for him to serve, and less likelihood that he will simply burn out, and he will avoid drifting into a self-righteous attitude where he thinks he's better than those who do less than he does.

When we're feeling down

We want each part of us to respond to God, and our feelings will take their place in that whole-person response.

But what about when I don't actually feel very much? What about when God seems far away, or my heart feels cold towards him, or I don't care about his Word, or when I feel nothing for his people and his work? Such times will come.

Keep reading because we're going to think in the second half of this book how we can cultivate right feelings. Keep reading because we'll see why we don't always feel, and we'll try to set realistic expectations. But for now I'm going to set our lack of feeling in the context of our whole-person response, and the simple answer to the questions in the above paragraph is to keep living for God.

We must keep believing God's Word, even when we don't feel the truth of it. We must keep living for God, even when we don't feel like it. This is why the Bible speaks about the need for self-control and perseverance – because there will be many times when we don't feel like doing the right thing. I'm not saying we should be happy with that. But I am saying that there will be times when that is the case in our lives.

Take Job in the Old Testament who went through the most appalling experiences – all his children were killed, and then he was horribly and painfully ill. He felt like he wished he'd never been born or that he had died at birth (see Job 3). He says,

> For sighing has become my daily food;
> my groans pour out like water.
> What I feared has come upon me;
> what I dreaded has happened to me.
> I have no peace, no quietness;
> I have no rest, but only turmoil.
> (Job 3:24–26)

He feels terrible! I don't know if you've ever been that down, felt that devastated. The temptation is then to turn against God. We're tempted to stop believing in God, or trusting in him; we certainly feel tempted not to live for God. That was Job's temptation.

So what does he do? It's a complicated story, but here's one verse describing his reaction: 'Though he slay me, yet will I hope in him' (Job 13:15). Job continues to trust in God no matter what. He is steadfast despite what he feels. He refuses to let his feelings drive his life; instead he continues to live in the light of the truth he already knows about God.

Here's another example from David. It's written at a time when he feels like God is very far away:

> How long, LORD? Will you forget me forever?
>   How long will you hide your face from me?
> How long must I wrestle with my thoughts
>   and day after day have sorrow in my heart?
> How long will my enemy triumph over me?
>   (Psalm 13:1–2)

It seems like God has forgotten all about him and gone into hiding. And so David is feeling pretty down – thoughts are going round and round in his mind, and his heart is full of sorrow day after day.

David goes on to call on God to act, but he then finishes the psalm with these amazing words:

> But I trust in your unfailing love;
>   my heart rejoices in your salvation.
> I will sing the LORD's praise,
>   for he has been good to me.
>   (Psalm 13:5–6)

David says he will continue to trust God, continue to rejoice in God, and even continue to sing to God. And this is before God has done anything; this is still while he's feeling down. David presses on in living for God, even when he doesn't feel like it.

David rejoices in God when he's not feeling joyful. First, his rejoicing is based on something: he says he will continue to sing because the Lord has been good to him. So he will rejoice in God for his goodness, even if he doesn't feel like it in the present. That's really important!

Christians know how incredibly good God has been to them. They know how God has loved them, forgiven them and adopted them. And we must live in the light of those truths, no matter what we feel God is doing in the present. Those truths mean we can continue to rejoice in God and sing to him 'for he has been good to me'.

This is one reason why Christians are called to be thankful 'in all circumstances' (1 Thessalonians 5:18). That is being thankful even when life is rubbish. It's not that we think the rubbish is actually good, but we still think God is good.

The second thing we must do is choose to have these attitudes. Within his sadness, David can choose to rejoice in God and sing to him. We need to be careful here. We saw earlier that we can't command emotion. I can't simply say to myself, 'Graham, be happy.' That's not how feelings work.

But we can choose how we direct and focus our thoughts. Here's a silly illustration. My wife and I went on a house-exchange holiday where we swapped houses with another couple (which is something we still do despite the details of this story!). When we arrived at their house, we were pretty disappointed – the setting wasn't great and the house was uninspiring. It got worse. We soon discovered that the place was dirty: the beds hadn't been changed, the floor hadn't been swept. It was as if the family had made absolutely no effort to clean up for our arrival. When my wife found rotting food in the fridge, we considered leaving.

We had a choice. We could focus on what was rubbish about this house and fume about it. Or we could clean up and within a couple of hours start getting on with our holiday. We chose to do the latter. We now look back and laugh about our arrival. We managed to have a good holiday in the end.

But we had to choose what attitude to adopt. We couldn't simply tell ourselves, 'Feel happy about this house.' But we could adopt a positive or a negative attitude towards it. We could sit around and grumble and feel more miserable. Or we could up and get on. And the result? We felt better about it.

Our culture often thinks we can't change our feelings. We resign ourselves to feeling down, flat, unsatisfied or whatever, until something comes along to change how we feel. David sets us an example – he chooses to rejoice at a moment when he feels sad; he sings praise at a time when he feels like singing the blues.

So when we're feeling down, there are lots of things we mustn't do. We mustn't give up on God; we mustn't stop trusting him; we mustn't stop living for him. And there are things we get on with – we rejoice in him and praise him anyway.

Beware: wrong use of emotions!

I hope you've seen that we should be really positive about our emotions. They are a wonderful part of how God has made us and they should be part of how we respond to God, and part of the Christ-like Christian life.

But emotions are not always right. Just like we can think wrongly, we can feel wrongly.

Used as a source of right and wrong

Our emotions aren't designed to tell us truth – truth about God, about ourselves, about salvation, or how to live. That truth comes to us from the Bible, and we get it first by using our minds to understand what God has said.

Of course it's not always that simple. I might feel guilty about something, while my mind is justifying myself and saying I didn't do anything wrong. My feelings might actually be telling me the truth. Or I might respond very emotionally to a tragic situation, and that reaction might be telling me more 'truth' about what's happened than my mind.

So I'm not saying our emotions never tell us anything in life. But I am saying that we mustn't let them take the place of the Bible. I remember Isabel. She told me that she really loved God and really wanted to live for him. But she was sleeping with her boyfriend. When asked why, she simply replied that it felt right and she couldn't deny her feelings. She was using her emotions to make decisions about how to live.

Adrian told me he couldn't believe in a God who would send people to hell. 'Why not?' I asked. 'Because it doesn't feel right,' he replied. He was using his feelings to decide truth about God.

Or we might make how we feel the measure of right and wrong in a dispute. I've dealt with a whole variety of fallings out and bust-ups in church life. We talk it through; we look for apologies, forgiveness and reconciliation. But within that process I sometimes hear people say, 'But he made me feel so angry.' Of course someone may have done something very wrong that rightly made them feel so angry. But often this is used as a piece of evidence: I felt very angry, so you must have been very wrong. That's using my feelings as a source of truth.

There are lots of other examples. We might decide not to challenge a Christian friend's wrong behaviour when we should.

We say, 'It didn't feel right', which is often a cover for 'I didn't want to because it would have felt awkward.' Or we might make feelings the measure of how good a sermon or a time of worship was: the best sermons make me feel challenged or comforted, the best worship makes me cry or smile. Of course good sermons and worship should affect how we feel, but how we feel is not the ultimate measure. Or we make our feelings the judge of our spiritual state: if I feel good, then all is well.

The Anglican preacher and revival leader John Wesley saw and encouraged many experiences of God. In the revivals in the eighteenth century, people were having all kinds of spiritual (and not-so-spiritual) experiences. Wesley gave this advice in a letter: 'You are not to judge by your own feelings, but by the word of God.'[2] He was right. If we judge by emotions only, we're standing on a very shaky foundation.

Used as an excuse

Sometimes we use our feelings to excuse something we know is wrong. It can often be in the sort of bust-up I have just mentioned. Someone feels really angry, and so they say or do something in the heat of the moment. It's like the flashpoint on the football pitch when the commentator says, 'He saw red.' They mean that the player was so overwhelmed by anger or frustration that he kicked out or hit someone. He did something which he knew was wrong. We too can lash out at someone in a sort of relational road rage.

We can surprise ourselves sometimes – our feelings can be so powerful. And not just feelings of anger or annoyance, but we can be overwhelmed with feelings of desire or jealousy or greed. And these can lead us to sin, which is why Paul says, 'In your anger do not sin' (Ephesians 4:26).

What we must not do then is use our feelings as an excuse: 'I did that because of how I felt.' Of course we did it because of how we felt, but that doesn't make it OK. We remain responsible for our actions; we can in fact exercise self-control. Don't misuse your emotions by using them as excuses.

Too much, or too little

Bob was really passionate about doctrine – about certain doctrines anyway. He felt really strongly about a small, obscure point to do with the return of Jesus. My concern was that Bob was more passionate about that than about really central doctrines, like Jesus' death. And if you challenged Bob, he'd simply say, 'But it's true; it's in the Bible, so I should feel strongly about it.' And the answer was, 'Yes, it is true, but not as important as other things.' Bob had got things out of perspective.

This is an example of too much feeling for something; making something more important than it is worth. We do this all the time. We take something that is true and right and good, but then make it the thing we feel most passionately about. What we feel must be in proportion to the significance of the issue, not just the rightness of the issue.

Looking for experience

We should be concerned about how we feel. But we shouldn't be looking for certain experiences. There are lots of dangers here. We can want to feel something more than we can want to be like Christ; we can want certain experiences more than we want to serve God; we can live for experience more than we live to glorify God. This is a misuse of our emotions. They are good things in their right place – but their right place is not as the goal of life.

Jonathan Edwards wrote about people who looked for, and delighted in, certain experiences. He tells us what they say to themselves:

'What a good experience is this! What a great discovery is this!
What wonderful things have I met with!' And so they put their
experiences in the place of Christ, and his beauty and fullness;
and instead of rejoicing in Christ Jesus, they rejoice in their
admirable experiences.[3]

Do you see how terrible this could be? We could rejoice in our
experiences instead of rejoicing in Jesus. We could replace
Jesus with feelings. If we make our aim simply to feel happy,
we'll focus on our feelings and lose sight of him.

Feeling without living

Remember Isabel above? She was sleeping with her boyfriend
and saying it was OK because it felt right. You might remember
that she also said she really loved God. And I don't doubt that
she felt a great deal towards God – great thankfulness and joy
and love. But I had to tell her that she didn't really love him.
I said so because of the words of Jesus: 'Anyone who loves me
will obey my teaching' (John 14:23). Any feeling that doesn't
result in living for Jesus isn't the real deal.

We need to be careful here because our feelings can run
ahead of our living. We can feel like we will love God totally,
but then find ourselves disobeying him. I remember a particular
church service that focused on mission. There were some inter-
views with mission partners; there was preaching on God's
heart for the world; there was passionate singing about serving
God in proclaiming the gospel. At the end of the service I felt
like signing up straight away! But I'd be the first to admit that
I haven't actually lived out that desire to serve God totally.

So we can feel 'above' what we live out. We can feel
something deeply, yet not act in line with it. But that doesn't
mean it wasn't a good and a right thing to feel. The abuse
we're concerned with here is a focus on feeling something

that has no effect on life, rather than whether it has a full effect. Isabel above wasn't trying not to sleep with her boyfriend and failing sometimes. She was happily pressing on in disobeying God while saying she felt great love for him. That's a misuse of emotions.

Good feelings become bad feelings

Feelings can be slippery things! Perfectly good and right feelings can easily slide into something else. So I should feel great concern for truth and right doctrine, but I must beware that that doesn't slide into arrogance or anger at those who disagree with me. I should feel hatred of sin and all its painful consequences, but I must watch out that that doesn't slide into hating the people who sin. I should admire and appreciate people's gifts and talents, but I must beware that that doesn't slide into becoming envious of them. I should delight to praise God in song, but I must beware that that doesn't become delight in music alone.

Emotions in perspective

This has been a chapter about perspective – emotions in their right place. Feelings take their place as part of a whole response to God; they're not the whole response themselves. They take their place in a life informed by God's Word through our minds and flowing out into a life lived for God in practice. We need to keep them where they belong.

Questions and ideas for reflection

1. Describe in your own words how thinking, feeling and acting should be connected in the Christian life.
2. Why should we be positive about thinking in the Christian life?

3. Why should we be positive about feeling in the Christian life?

4. Why should we be positive about acting in the Christian life?

5. How do you tend to respond to God when you are feeling down? How might you want to change that?

6. Which misuse of emotions are you most prone to?

part 2
emotions in
practice

part 2
emotions in
practice

6
emotions and the Bible

God made us to live life in full emotional colour, and so we want to recalibrate our hearts to love the right things and hate the wrong things. Our key tool here is God's Word, the Bible.

God's Word tells us how things really are. It tells us what is truly good and what is evil, what should be valued and what should be rejected, what we should rejoice in and what we should cry over, what we should get angry about and what we should let go. It tells us about God and his goodness, and how we should feel about him. It tells us about ourselves and our sin and how we should feel about it.

> *Right thinking from God's Word lies behind right feeling.*

It tells us about God's salvation and future promises, and how we should think and feel about them. Right thinking from God's Word lies behind right feeling.

So we need to be taught God's Word well. We need to be in churches that teach us thoroughly, in small groups where we can discuss what we believe, and we need to be reading God's Word for ourselves. This is a basic part of Christian growth and a basic part of growth in godly feelings.

From head to heart

Knowing that salvation should bring me joy is one thing, but how do I feel it? Knowing I shouldn't be angry with someone doesn't stop me bubbling with rage. We also need to get Bible truths deeper into us; they need to drop from our heads to our hearts.

One answer to this is meditation. That word might conjure up images of people sitting cross-legged and humming. But that's not what it's about. Meditation in the Bible is about chewing on God's Word and absorbing it:

> I remember the days of long ago;
>> I meditate on all your works
>> and consider what your hands have done.
>
> (Psalm 143:5)

There are three things which David says he's doing: he's remembering, meditating and considering. He is looking back at what God has done in the past and remembering it, reflecting on it and considering all he has done. The Hebrew word for 'meditation' used here has the idea of speaking to yourself or muttering under your breath. David is saying that he's going to remember what God has done by repeating it to himself, and as he says it over and over to himself, he will think about it.

Here's another example:

I meditate on your precepts
  and consider your ways.
(Psalm 119:15)

This one is about considering or thinking over something. It's turning something over in your mind. When the psalmist goes on to say he'll 'consider [God's] ways', this conveys the idea of looking closely at them. It's like picking up a gemstone and turning it over in your hand, examining it and studying it closely. That's what he is doing here.

Also:

Within your temple, O God,
  we meditate on your unfailing love.
(Psalm 48:9)

Here what is being meditated on isn't God's commands or actions, but his character – his unfailing love. A different word is used again which conveys the idea of comparing, thinking about, what God's love is like, and asking, 'What is it like? What shall I compare it to?'

Do you grasp the idea of meditation? Repeating, thinking, considering and taking in. What is being meditated on? God's actions, God's commands and God's character. This is not teaching. The psalmist knows what God has done, what he's commanded and what he is like. But now he is meditating on those things in order to absorb them and take them into his heart.

I love watching rugby, especially England. I remember watching one particular game when England were playing the All Blacks. England were expected to lose – the All Blacks were so much better, and England hadn't been playing well. But amazingly, wonderfully, they won. (It wasn't a pretty game, mind you.) And I enjoyed that game so much.

I watched the game live with some friends. But I'd recorded it as well, and the next day I watched it again. My wife asked, 'Why are you watching that? You saw it yesterday.' I replied that I wanted to go over it, look at how we had won it, consider it all and celebrate it. You could say that I meditated on that game. There was repetition, considering and reflecting. I didn't learn anything new, but I appreciated it all the more.

That's what we get out of meditation. We don't learn new truths; we understand old truths more deeply. It is about depth of absorption rather than superficial awareness. The Puritan minister Richard Baxter said this about meditation: 'Meditation does, as it were, open the door between the head and the heart.'[1]

So I know I should be glad about forgiveness, I know I should be in awe of God and I know I should rejoice in my future hope. I know I should, but I don't. So I need to meditate.

Promoting the positive

We can approach meditation in two ways. First, we can be proactive and promote what we want to see in our lives. We want to feel joy in our relationship with God, so we meditate on the truth of his goodness to us; we want to feel peace, so we meditate on his sovereign care. We help to cultivate what should be there by meditating on truth.

Here's an example of David speaking to himself:

Praise the LORD, my soul;
    all my inmost being, praise his holy name.
(Psalm 103:1)

David is calling himself to praise God, saying, 'Come on, soul, praise the Lord!' You probably know you should praise God, but what about when you don't feel like doing it? We can begin like David by just telling ourselves to get on with it. But that's not all David does. He gives himself reasons to praise God, meditating on all that God has done for him:

> Praise the LORD, my soul,
>   and forget not all his benefits –
> who forgives all your sins
>   and heals all your diseases,
> who redeems your life from the pit
>   and crowns you with love and compassion,
> who satisfies your desires with good things
>   so that your youth is renewed like the eagle's.
> (Psalm 103:2–5)

He is listing all God's 'benefits', all the things God does for him. He's reflecting on all God's actions to him, telling himself truth about God, to lead himself to praise him.

And that's how the psalm continues. It contains some fabulous truths:

> The LORD works righteousness
>   and justice for all the oppressed.
>
> He made known his ways to Moses,
>   his deeds to the people of Israel:
> The LORD is compassionate and gracious,
>   slow to anger, abounding in love.
> He will not always accuse,
>   nor will he harbour his anger forever;
> he does not treat us as our sins deserve
>   or repay us according to our iniquities.
> For as high as the heavens are above the earth,
>   so great is his love for those who fear him;

as far as the east is from the west,
    so far has he removed our transgressions from us.
(Psalm 103:6–12)

What great things to tell yourself! Truths about God's character – his compassion and grace and love. Truths about God's actions that flow from that character: his forgiveness and the removal of our sin.

David goes on:

As a father has compassion on his children,
    so the LORD has compassion on those who fear him;
for he knows how we are formed,
    he remembers that we are dust.
The life of mortals is like grass,
    they flourish like a flower of the field;
the wind blows over it and it is gone,
    and its place remembers it no more.
But from everlasting to everlasting
    the LORD's love is with those who fear him,
    and his righteousness with their children's children –
with those who keep his covenant
    and remember to obey his precepts.

The LORD has established his throne in heaven,
    and his kingdom rules over all.
(Psalm 103:13–19)

David reminds himself of God's compassion for us – like the best father we could think of. He reminds himself how fleeting and brief our life is, but that God's love is constant, certain and with us for ever. He reminds himself of God's rule and kingdom.

And so he finishes by calling everyone everywhere to praise God:

> Praise the LORD, you his angels,
>> you mighty ones who do his bidding,
>> who obey his word.
> Praise the LORD, all his heavenly hosts,
>> you his servants who do his will.
> Praise the LORD, all his works
>> everywhere in his dominion.
>
> Praise the LORD, my soul.
> (Psalm 103:20–22)

The last line is the same as the first. Do you think David said it with more feeling and conviction at the end? I do. Having covered all this ground, having reflected on such great truths about God, I would be shouting at the end, 'Praise the Lord, my soul!'

David didn't tell himself anything new though. He was dwelling on old truths. It was an exercise in getting his heart to praise God by meditating on him.

That's an example of promoting what we want to see in our emotional life. We want to see peace, joy, thankfulness, love and fear of God. Not because we're seeking those feelings because they feel nice, but because we want to live in the light of who God is and what he's done.

So what might we do in practice? Think of a good and right emotion or heart attitude that you want to develop and grow in, thankfulness for example. And then not only tell yourself to be thankful, but also meditate on Bible truths that lie behind thankfulness. Think of writing your own poem / song that would encourage thankfulness, like David did. Turn to Bible verses that speak about thankfulness, and dwell on them, repeating their truths and considering them carefully.

Combatting the negative

Secondly, we can be reactive and combat what is negative. We know we are feeling down, unloved, proud, self-pitying, anxious or whatever. And rather than just living with those feelings, we can respond by choosing a truth of God to counter those feelings, and meditate on it.

A great example is Psalm 77. It is written by a guy called Asaph at a time of distress and desperation:

> I cried out to God for help;
>> I cried out to God to hear me.
> When I was in distress, I sought the Lord;
>> at night I stretched out untiring hands,
>> and I would not be comforted.
> (Psalm 77:1–2)

He goes on to talk about how desperate he is. As he thinks about God, he groans; he can't sleep; he is too troubled even to speak; he thinks back to how things used to be when he was happy and sang to God. This guy is not in good shape. Maybe you can think of times like that, times when troubles overwhelmed you, times when you thought you would never smile again.

Asaph starts to ask questions of God:

> 'Will the Lord reject forever?
>> Will he never show his favour again?
> Has his unfailing love vanished forever?
>> Has his promise failed for all time?

Has God forgotten to be merciful?
    Has he in anger withheld his compassion?'
(Psalm 77:7–9)

Has God turned his back on me? That's how Asaph feels. He expresses it really strongly, asking where God's 'unfailing love' has gone. Have God's certain promises failed? Was all he knew to be true about God actually a dream? Had he been deceived?

I think of two people I met yesterday. Both of them are in hard situations. They feel desperately sad, confused and angry. In hard and tragic situations this is what it feels like. It feels as if God has left us. It feels like God was lying when he promised to love us.

We need to be honest and say that this is what it can feel like.

But we mustn't stay there. Asaph doesn't.

We see a change:

Then I thought, 'To this I will appeal:
    the years when the Most High stretched out his right hand.
I will remember the deeds of the LORD;
    yes, I will remember your miracles of long ago.
I will consider all your works
    and meditate on all your mighty deeds.'
(Psalm 77:10–12)

A thought comes to Asaph – he will look back. He will look back on what God has done. He will remember God's actions. He will consider and meditate on God's deeds.

And that's exactly what he does. The rest of the psalm is a rehearsal of the exodus where God brought his people out of Egypt. Asaph tells himself what God did then, and what God is like:

Your ways, God, are holy.
    What god is as great as our God?
You are the God who performs miracles;
    you display your power among the peoples.
With your mighty arm you redeemed your people,
    the descendants of Jacob and Joseph.

The waters saw you, God,
    the waters saw you and writhed;
    the very depths were convulsed.
The clouds poured down water,
    the heavens resounded with thunder;
    your arrows flashed back and forth.
Your thunder was heard in the whirlwind,
    your lightning lit up the world;
    the earth trembled and quaked.
Your path led through the sea,
    your way through the mighty waters,
    though your footprints were not seen.
You led your people like a flock
    by the hand of Moses and Aaron.
(Psalm 77:13–20)

Again, Asaph knew this stuff about the exodus before he started meditating. But he was dwelling on the past, bringing it to mind, turning it over in his head. He was getting truth into his heart.

We don't actually know how he felt at the end. That's where the psalm ends.

It would be great if Asaph had said, 'Then I felt like God was close and real and that he loved me.' But he doesn't; he doesn't say anything. There are examples in the Bible of where reflection and meditation do result in a change of feeling, but I've used this one to show that there's no guarantee of what perspective we'll gain and what emotions we'll have.

But there is the insistence that this was the right thing to do. When feeling like God had left, he needed to tell himself how God had acted in the past. When feeling like God was untrue to his promises and his character, he needed to remind himself what God was truly like.

> *When feeling like God had left, he needed to tell himself how God had acted in the past.*

We too need to meditate on truth. What might my two friends who feel so troubled say to themselves? What history might they repeat?

Here are some ideas:

- That God loved them so much that he sent Jesus to die for them (John 3:16)
- That God saved them not because of righteous things they'd done, but because of his mercy (Titus 3:5)
- That Jesus loved them and gave himself for them (Galatians 2:20)
- That God demonstrated his love for them by sending Jesus to die while they were still sinners (Romans 5:8)
- That God has sent his Spirit so they can know him as Father (Galatians 4:6)

They won't learn anything new. But they'll remind themselves of what is true, calling to mind reality.

That's what meditation is all about: from head to heart.

Reading the Bible in colour

And that's not the only connection between the Bible and our emotions. We also need to think about reading the Bible generally, or having it taught to us.

We often say that the Bible is written to teach us – and that's bang on; it is. But we often think that that means it's written to give us statements of truth. Statements like, 'God is love' or 'We are sinners' or 'Jesus died for us'. Well, you can find those actual statements in the Bible! But the Bible isn't simply full of bare statements. It comes in all different types and genres of writing, like history, poetry, letters, and much more. And it is written to motivate us to action and make us feel.

The content of a psalm can often be summed up in a few lines. But it's poetry, and so says the same thing in slightly different ways, repeating itself and using different pictures.

I've just opened the Psalms at random, and my eyes fell on Psalm 68:

May God arise, may his enemies be scattered;
  may his foes flee before him.
May you blow them away like smoke –
  as wax melts before the fire,
  may the wicked perish before God.
But may the righteous be glad
  and rejoice before God;
may they be happy and joyful.
(Psalm 68:1–3)

This is basically saying two things: may God's enemies be destroyed, and may the righteous be happy. That's all. But the psalm takes its time to say it. And it uses lots of pictures. Enemies are blown away like smoke, or they melt before God like a wax candle does in front of a fire.

This is not just a bare truth, but intended to make us feel something.

All literature makes us feel something – we might feel excitement at a thriller, longing at a poem or boredom at a textbook (not that they were aiming at that; they just hit it anyway!). The Bible is meant to make us feel something, not just know something. In fact it would be better to say it is written to make us know something, and so feel something and so do something.

So we don't simply read the Bible for information, and then have to go away and work on the feelings. Not at all. The feelings come as part of the package.

Of course this will vary from passage to passage. Some parts of Scripture are straightforward; some are more evocative. But we should always ask, 'What should this make me feel?'

Reading Genesis 1 and the account of creation should result in a feeling of wonder and awe at God's creative power and control. And also a feeling of privilege that we are made in his image. Reading the book of Judges and seeing the repeated cycle of sin should make us feel frustrated and angry at rebellion. Reading Jesus' cries from the cross should bring tears to our eyes. Reading of the faithfulness of the church in Smyrna in Revelation 2 should stiffen our resolve to stand for Christ.

As we read the Bible, ask yourself, 'What should I feel here?' as well as asking, 'What should I know?' and 'What should I do?' Ask all three, and connect all three together.

Given words to speak

We can use the Bible's words to help us to speak to God. Earlier I encouraged the idea of meditating on reasons to be thankful to him. But often we don't quite know where to start, or we quickly run out of steam. The solution is simple: use the Bible.

In particular, use the Psalms. The really unique thing about the Psalms is that they are words given by God, to be spoken to him. Not every psalm is expressed directly to God; some are to other people or to ourselves. But they are all about God. So this is God giving us words to speak. Words to speak back to him, words to speak to one another, words to say to ourselves. Make full use of the words God has given you.

So suppose we want to grow in our thankfulness:

> I will give thanks to you, LORD, with all my heart;
>   I will tell of all your wonderful deeds.
> I will be glad and rejoice in you;
>   I will sing the praises of your name, O Most High.
> (Psalm 9:1–2)

Make those words your own. Turn them into a prayer. Start to expand on them. Maybe say something like this: 'I will thank you God with all my heart; I'll speak about your wonderful deeds; everything you've done is wonderful, and you've done those wonderful things for me. So I want to thank you with all my heart. I will be glad and rejoice in you. I have such joy because of your kindness to me. I will sing praise to you. I want to lift your name high and give thanks to you because you are the Most High God.'

See the idea?

God has given us words to use, so let's use them. They are great words because they are true. And they are great because they encourage us to express right feelings to God, and to stir up those feelings.

Of course it doesn't have to be a psalm:

. . . giving joyful thanks to the Father, who has qualified you to share in the inheritance of his holy people in the kingdom of light. For he has rescued us from the dominion of darkness and brought us into the kingdom of the Son he loves, in whom we have redemption, the forgiveness of sins.
(Colossians 1:12–14)

This is part of Paul's prayer for the Colossians. Turn it into your prayer. Add to it. Expand on it. Maybe say something like: 'Father, please help me give thanks to you. Not just thanks but joyful thanks. I want to thank you because you have qualified me to share in the inheritance of your people – what a wonderful thing! I want to thank you because you've rescued me from the kingdom of darkness – that's where I was – and brought me into the kingdom of Jesus – that's where I am now. In him I have redemption; my sins have been forgiven. Thank you for these things. Please may I rejoice in them and be so grateful for them.'

Again, using these words helps us to express our feelings and stir up our feelings.

I'm not saying there's anything magical about using the words of the Bible. You might pray a prayer very similar to those above without even opening your Bible. But often we don't pray much about how we feel, or express emotion to God, and when we do we quickly run out of ideas (well, I do anyway). And so the above can be very helpful.

Of course it doesn't even have to be expressed in a prayer. I can simply use words of Scripture to speak truth to myself.

Jeff's story

One of my ongoing sins is pride. It's like one of those kids' toys where you hit a button down, but when you do so, another

button pops up somewhere else. I keep on hitting my pride, and
then realizing it's popped up in another form somewhere else.

But what I've found really helpful is using the words of
Daniel 4. They come from King Nebuchadnezzar who had
been proud, but God had humbled him. This is what
Nebuchadnezzar eventually says about God:

> His dominion is an eternal dominion;
>   his kingdom endures from generation to generation.
> All the peoples of the earth
>   are regarded as nothing.
> He does as he pleases
>   with the powers of heaven
>   and the peoples of the earth.
> No one can hold back his hand
>   or say to him: 'What have you done?'
> (Daniel 4:34–35)

I quite often just say these words over to myself slowly and
expand on them to get some perspective. God is big and I'm
small.

The fully feeling Bible reader

Unfortunately, in the Christian world we've managed to
develop a view where someone known for their love and deep
study of the Bible is thought of as dry and academic, not full
of feeling. What a disaster! It should be the other way round.
Good knowledge of the Bible brings good feelings. Meditation
on the Bible warms our hearts. Reading the Bible fills us with
awe and love. Using the words of the Bible helps us to express
our feelings and stirs them up within us.

Have a go!

Questions and suggestions for reflection

1. Do you struggle with getting knowledge from your head to your heart? Why?
2. What do you think of the idea of meditation?
3. Try meditating on a truth in order to develop a positive attitude and feeling.
4. Try meditating on a truth in order to combat a negative attitude and feeling.
5. What difference should feelings make in reading the Bible?
6. What do you want to change in this area in your own Bible reading?
7. Try turning a Bible prayer into your own prayer.

7
emotions and God's praise

I have two very clear memories of praise. One is of attending a stiff, suit-wearing ministers' conference in England where obscure hymns were sung with no musical accompaniment at all. We sang each hymn and immediately sat down. The other memory is of a charismatic church in Costa Rica. The band numbered about twenty, including three drummers. They loved singing and nothing would stop them!

Two very different scenes, but actually the same thing was happening in both of them. We were singing God's praise.

When Christians gather they praise God together in song. That's been true all through the Bible and it's been true all through church history. The Bible of course comes complete with a hymn book in the form of the Psalms. (Well, not exactly a hymn book, but close enough.)

And the reason is that God's people are told to sing:

Sing the praises of the LORD, you his faithful people;
   praise his holy name.
(Psalm 30:4)

Sing praises to God, sing praises;
   sing praises to our King, sing praises.
For God is the King of all the earth;
   sing to him a psalm of praise.
(Psalm 47:6–7)

[Speak] to one another with psalms, hymns, and songs from the
Spirit. Sing and make music from your heart to the Lord, always
giving thanks to God the Father for everything, in the name of
our Lord Jesus Christ.
(Ephesians 5:19–20)

God's people are a singing people!

And here's the point for all of us: singing is an emotional
activity. An emotional activity that God encourages us to
engage in.

Let's think about what is happening when we sing.

What exactly are we doing when we sing?

If we look through the Psalms, we find that people are doing
many, many different things as they sing. Here are some
examples:

- Expressing love, e.g. 'I love you, LORD, my strength'
  (Psalm 18:1)
- Stating a commitment, e.g. 'In you, LORD my God, I put
  my trust' (Psalm 25:1)

- Calling on God, e.g. 'Deliver me from my enemies, O God; be my fortress against those who are attacking me' (Psalm 59:1)
- Confessing sin, e.g. 'Have mercy on me, O God, according to your unfailing love; according to your great compassion blot out my transgressions' (Psalm 51:1)
- Questioning God, e.g. 'How long, LORD? Will you forget me forever? How long will you hide your face from me?' (Psalm 13:1)
- Calling other people to praise, e.g. 'Ascribe to the LORD the glory due his name; bring an offering and come into his courts' (Psalm 96:8)
- Encouraging people to give thanks to God, e.g. 'Give thanks to the LORD, for he is good; his love endures forever' (Psalm 118:29)
- Telling others how to live, e.g. 'Today, if only you would hear his voice, "Do not harden your hearts as you did at Meribah"' (Psalm 95:7–8)
- Stating truth, e.g. 'Blessed are those who have regard for the weak; the LORD delivers them in times of trouble' (Psalm 41:1)
- Repeating historical facts, e.g. 'When Israel came out of Egypt, Jacob from a people of foreign tongue . . . ' (Psalm 114:1)
- Praising God for personal blessings, e.g. 'I will sing the LORD's praise, for he has been good to me' (Psalm 13:6)
- Rejoicing in God for helping us, e.g. 'I will be glad and rejoice in your love, for you saw my affliction and knew the anguish of my soul' (Psalm 31:7)
- Encouraging ourselves, e.g. 'Praise the LORD, my soul; all my inmost being, praise his holy name' (Psalm 103:1)

You get the idea. We're speaking in a variety of directions: to God, to one another, to ourselves. It is all about God of course, all to do with him, but it is to do with him in lots of different ways. To put it another way, in singing we are expressing various aspects of our whole relationship with God. That's one of the reasons why it's hard to give it a single label like 'praise' or 'worship' because we're doing more than just praising or worshipping God. And of course we praise and worship God in many other ways as well as by singing. (I'm using those terms because there aren't any others to use, but am aware they're not ideal.)

This wide spectrum of what's happening when we sing is important because it means that there's no mystery about singing. We're expressing the normal stuff of relating to God: confessing sin, expressing thanks, asking for help. In that sense there's nothing special about 'praise' or 'worship'.

So why do we sing?

So the question is, what's the difference between singing and just saying? The fact is that music engages our feelings. We say that we are moved by a piece of music; it has that ability to stir us emotionally. And when we're singing to and about God, it is appropriate for us to be stirred emotionally. Remember what we've been saying we're doing in singing: rejoicing, praising, thanking, confessing, asking, and more. Those are all things which we should feel something about.

And so we sing for two reasons. First, it allows us to *express* our emotion. This is why joy and praise in the Psalms are so often connected with singing:

I will be glad and rejoice in you;
    I will sing the praises of your name, O Most High.
(Psalm 9:2)

There's an expression of heart attitude to God – gladness and joy – which is then expressed in song. And we can express how we feel towards God better, if we're given good words set to a good tune. The great hymn writer Isaac Watts said,

> Let us remember, that the very power of singing was given to human nature chiefly for this purpose, that our own warmest affections of soul might break out into natural or divine melody, and that the tongue of the worshipper might express his own heart.[1]

Secondly, singing *stirs* our emotions. It can help arouse the appropriate response in me. I can't show you a Bible verse that says that directly, but I believe it makes sense. To put it differently, we all know that music is powerful, and God has made it so. So I sing to harness that power in my relationship with God. Jonathan Edwards said,

> . . . the duty of singing praises to God seems to be appointed wholly to excite and express religious affections. No other reason can be assigned why we should express ourselves to God in verse, rather than in prose, and do it with music but only, that such is our nature and frame, that these things have a tendency to move our affections.[2]

We sing both to express and to stir up our emotions. That means that praise is a tool for growing in godly feelings, and a major way in which we express godly feelings.

Implications

There are some big implications here. First, this means we shouldn't be afraid of our feelings being stirred up by praise. In some quarters people say, 'Don't worry about feeling anything; that's all frothy emotion anyway.' In fact, occasionally times of singing are organized in such a way that seems specifically designed to keep emotion at bay. (OK, there are some dangers, but these mustn't prevent us from allowing ourselves to feel.)

Secondly, we must see that in praise we are not simply chasing feelings themselves. What we want to feel is what fits with what we are singing. There is, or should be, a link between the feeling in my heart and the truth in my mind being spoken by my lips. So if I am speaking of the joy of salvation, I want to stir up and express joy. In confessing sin, I want to stir up and express sorrow. In stating truth, I want to stir up and express conviction.

I worry that some people don't expect or want to feel anything in singing. And I worry that other people don't care what they feel in singing, as long as they feel something. We don't want singing that is either heartless or mindless.

We don't want singing that is either heartless or mindless.

Thirdly, the power of music means we need to be careful how we sing. We want our feelings to come because of the truth, not the music. The music should be an aid to my feeling, not the source. So again there is a challenge to engage with what we're singing and not simply get carried away by the tune, for if we do, we can start worshipping 'worship', where we delight in feeling and not in God.

John Calvin said that music has 'the greatest value in kindling our hearts to a true zeal and eagerness to pray'. Absolutely right. But he went on to say, 'Yet we should be very careful that our ears be not more attentive to the melody than our minds to the spiritual meaning of the words.'[3] At the end of a time of praise I should not be left saying, 'That was great!' but 'God is great!'

There are implications also for how times of praise are put together and how they are led, especially in terms of what is appropriate and helpful. And that's where the debate starts: how do we draw the distinction between what is helpful to stir and express emotion and what is musical manipulation? That's a complicated area.

At the end of a time of praise I should not be left saying, 'That was great!' but 'God is great!'

There are cultural issues at play here too. My two different experiences at the beginning of this chapter illustrate this. You might have thought that the stiff hymn-singing crowd were down on emotion. But you'd be wrong. They sang with great passion; there was a profound sense of awe and worship.

Latin American culture on the other hand meant having three drummers, everyone jumping up and down, and singing for an hour at a time was normal! But someone from the 'stiff' conference might have said this was emotional manipulation. The answer isn't that there is some 'ideal' middle position, so that the stiff Brits should warm up, and the excitable Latins should cool down. No, culture simply varies.

So while there is such a thing as emotional manipulation through music, you simply cannot define by the style of singing, the size of the band, the length of the songs and so on when it is happening. It is a much more subtle thing.

In fact, it can only really be detected by the worshipping individual. Even within any one culture, a particular style of singing can be appropriately helpful for one person but manipulative for someone else. The question to ask ourselves is why I feel what I feel. In particular, are my feelings connected to the content of what I'm singing? Could you replace the words of the song with any old words and still feel the same?

While these are significant issues to think through, we mustn't miss the big point. As we gather to sing together with God's people, we express and stir up right and godly emotions. Pray for that to happen at your church and for you personally. For all of us, each church gathering should be a time of greater understanding and reminding of truth about God, and a time of greater passion and warmth of heart for God.

Such a good experience

I was a visiting preacher and we had a time of praise before I spoke. The person who introduced me at the service began by saying, 'Wow, you just get lost in that worship, don't you?' There was a general murmur of agreement from around the room. And I thought to myself, 'But what about if you didn't feel "lost" in it?' What if you don't feel what others do?

This can be a real issue. It can easily lead people to feel like they're second-class Christians, or even not Christians at all. Or if the person with the great experience is in the minority, he or she can be made to feel unusual and odd.

First, we need to realize that different personalities, backgrounds and upbringings come into play here (as we saw in a previous chapter). They are not the source of our feelings, but they do mean that some of us feel more easily and more deeply than others. That fact alone means we would expect a variety of experience among us in any congregation.

Secondly, we may be in different places spiritually. I once broke down crying during a time of praise. But I know that it had a lot to do with what God was doing and teaching me at that time. Several things came together as I sang (and I was quite tired which means that I cry more easily). We don't all expect to have exactly the same reaction to a sermon, because some of us might be challenged, whereas others of us might be comforted. The same variety can happen in praise.

But I think a major issue here is what we think is happening when we sing. As I said above, some people think not much is happening – it's just a warm-up to the main event, the sermon. They may even want to avoid feeling anything, and so they won't speak in terms of any 'experience'.

My challenge here is to say that we are doing significant business with God when we sing, calling on him, rejoicing in his goodness, celebrating his salvation, and more. And expressing emotion in these is right. I'd encourage those who think differently to develop a higher view of praise.

But there are wrong views of praise which encourage a wrong view of experience in it. Probably the most common idea here is that in singing we are entering God's presence. You see this on the back of CDs of praise music. One describes 'songs that provide an avenue for the listener to enter into the presence of the Lord'. Or another says that by listening I will 'experience the manifest presence of God'.

I'm not trying to knock the idea of emotion in praise, but the idea that music is the means by which I get transported into God's presence. If you take what these CDs say seriously, the music is like an escalator that takes me up to God. But we already have access to God through Jesus, by the Spirit, so we don't actually need background music.

What some people mean by those phrases is that, when they reflect on God's truth in song, it's very meaningful to them. And that is great, what I've been arguing for. But to say that praise lifts me into another realm of experience of God is in danger of denying the truth of the gospel that we already have access to God through Jesus.

Worship leader Bob Kauflin writes of times when we may experience a wave of peace or a rise of irrepressible joy while singing. And then he says, 'In those moments has God's presence come down to us? Have we been led into God's presence? No. God was present from the beginning. We've just become more aware of it.'[4] And so my challenge to those who speak of great experiences in worship is: make sure you're not turning singing into something it shouldn't be.

The most helpful thing is to be clear on what we're aiming for. It's very easy in these discussions to think that it's all about a certain depth of feeling or a certain height of experience. It's not. We want praise of God that involves reality, reality of knowledge of God, reality of response to God. And that will mean reality of feeling.

Jonathan Edwards spoke about people's experience of God in times of great revival, when amazing events were reported. One of his key marks of godly affections was that they should be connected with true understanding, and so he said people should not be aiming at experience but at reality of engagement with God:

> The child of God is graciously affected, because he sees and understands something more of divine things than he did before, more of God or Christ and of the glorious things exhibited in the gospel; he has some clearer and better view than he had before, when he was not affected: either he receives some understanding of divine things that is new to him; or has his former knowledge renewed after the view was decayed.[5]

To sum it up, he says there should never be 'heat without light' – feeling without understanding. But unfortunately there can be. Many occasions can bring very profound and even ecstatic experiences. But the height of the experience doesn't make it a good thing. We're aiming at reality of engagement with God, and that doesn't dictate what depths or heights of feeling we need to have.

Questions for reflection

1. Do you enjoy singing praise to God? Why or why not?
2. What difference does it make to be aware of the different things we are doing when we sing?
3. Is singing 'special'? What makes it different from repeating truth without music?
4. What dangers are you aware of for yourself in praise?
5. What is your attitude to other people's experience of praise? Do you need to change this?
6. How do you want to change in the way you engage in praise?

8
emotions and the church

'No-one can tell me what I should feel.'

'No-one understands how I feel.'

Emotions are very personal things. Only I can feel what I am currently feeling. But in our culture today we are encouraged to focus on 'me and my feelings', so we make statements like the ones above.

But in the church it can't be like that. Here other people get involved in my emotions, and I get involved in theirs. It's messy, but it's part of real church.

Made for community

We are made to relate. It's part of being made in the image of God. God himself lives in a loving community, in three persons in one 'family'. And when he makes us in his image, he makes us to live in loving community with one another, as well under him as our King and God.

That's the original design. But it was shattered in the fall, when we turned against God (Genesis 3). The big result was that we were out of relationship with God – pictured by Adam and Eve being thrown out of the Garden of Eden. But there was another result: our relationships with one another were wrecked as well.

So instead of loving community, we now have Adam and Eve blaming each other. In the very next chapter after the fall (Genesis 4) we have hatred between two brothers, leading to the first murder. Sin had wrecked community. And it's because of sin that we have envy, hatred, lust, accusation, suspicion, pride, selfishness, racism, bitterness, and everything else that messes up our relationship with one another.

But through the work of Jesus, God reconciles us back to him – and to one another. In Ephesians 2, Paul says that one of Jesus' purposes in dying was to bring peace between people, to reconcile them to one another (Ephesians 2:15–16). Now as we come to trust in Jesus and are saved, we are also joined to his people, the church. We come under God as our Father, and we join his people as our family.

We grow in godly feelings, express godly feelings, and live out the fully feeling life, in community.

So what? And why are we discussing the church in a book on emotions?

Lots of reasons!

We live out the Christian life as part of our new family, part of a local church. And just like it takes a family to raise a child, it takes a church to raise a Christian. We think much too easily of Christian growth as an individual thing: *I* grow in *my* understanding and *my* living for God. And now, having got so far in this book, maybe we would add, *I* grow in *my* godly feelings. Wrong.

Growth in godly feelings is not an individual exercise; no part of Christian growth is. Left to ourselves, we won't get very far. We grow in godly feelings, express godly feelings, and live out the fully feeling life, in community.

Spurring one another on

God's people are to teach us God's truth and encourage us in it. We are to spur one another on in the Christian life. And that will, or should, include our godly feelings.

In the letter to the Hebrews we read, 'And let us consider how we may spur one another on toward love and good deeds, not giving up meeting together, as some are in the habit of doing, but encouraging one another – and all the more as you see the Day approaching' (Hebrews 10:24–25). Some people thought they could keep going as Christians by themselves, and so they'd stopped meeting with other Christians. (There was the possibility of persecution, so they had some reason for not going to church, but it was still a very bad call.) However, we can't make it on our own. We need to keep one another going.

Here we are to keep one another going in 'love' for one another and 'good deeds' towards one another. That love involves more than feelings (we've said that already), but it does involve how I feel towards my Christian brothers and sisters.

So here's the point: we are to spur one another on in this love, and in the good deeds that will follow. I should get on with loving people myself, but I also need other people to help me stir up that love, to tell me how Jesus has made us family, how we're to reflect his love for one another, how God has first loved us, so we too should love one another, how we are one body in Christ.

Kate's story

I was finding someone in our small group really annoying – not just annoying, *really* annoying. When we shared stuff for prayer, this person kept on going on about his problems, which never really changed, and didn't seem all that bad in the first place. I just wanted to scream, 'Get a grip!' It started showing when I began making little comments, snide criticisms.

Anyway, I ended up talking to our group leaders. We chatted about that person, his background, why he was like that. We chatted about how we had to bear with one another and be patient with one another. We chatted about how family life is full of those sorts of tensions, and we should think of our group as family. We chatted about how God has shown his love and patience to us when we're really annoying.

So, he's still annoying, but I think I'm now doing better at trying to love him.

Earlier in Hebrews we read about helping one another with our attitude towards God: 'See to it, brothers and sisters, that none of you has a sinful, unbelieving heart that turns away from the living God. But encourage one another daily, as long as it is called "Today," so that none of you may be hardened by sin's deceitfulness' (Hebrews 3:12–13). The concern is that we might turn away from God, that our hearts might be deceived by sin and become hard towards God. That's a real possibility for us, and it's scary.

Now this passage is about our whole attitude to God, not specifically our feelings. But these come into play too. It's an issue of whether our hearts are warm to God or growing cold. It's about whether we are rejoicing in our salvation or moaning about it. It's more than what we say we believe or how we live.

So how will we prevent having these cold, hard hearts? What's the answer?

'Encourage one another . . . '

The answer for each one of us lies in other people encouraging us. And we too are part of the answer for others as we encourage them.

Now this is not the usual 'Well done, that was great' type. Encouragement in the book of Hebrews is speaking truth about Jesus to one another so that we're encouraged to keep trusting and loving him. It's telling one another how brilliant Jesus is, how great his work of salvation is, what we now have and what we look forward to in Jesus.

We want churches where believers are helping to keep one another's hearts warm towards God and rejoicing in Jesus. If you take a piece of coal out of the fire and leave it by itself, it will quickly stop burning and cool down, but if it's kept together with the other coals, then it will burn on. It's a well-worn illustration, but it's true: we Christians keeping one another burning.

We can also see this spurring on in specific areas of the Christian life. In the small town of Thessalonica, Paul had to teach the church what had happened to Christians who had died. He wanted to assure them that they shouldn't grieve like the rest of the world does (1 Thessalonians 4:13). He doesn't mean they shouldn't grieve at all – but that within that grieving there is hope. And he goes on to speak about the return of Christ, the completion of salvation and the joy of being with the Lord.

Paul finishes with this: 'Therefore encourage one another with these words' (1 Thessalonians 4:18).

So picture what Paul wants to happen. Mary's mum has died, and she is grieving – rightly so. But Paul wants Dawn and James to call round to Mary, to sympathize with her and encourage her, to remind her of our hope in Jesus. So Mary ends up feeling different.

Have you had the experience of talking with someone and being encouraged by it? Maybe you began by feeling flat or anxious about an issue, or grieving the loss of a friend or a relative. And after an hour of tea and chat, although the situation hadn't changed, you left feeling better. You felt more positive, more at peace, whatever.

What happened? A friend encouraged you. Helped you get perspective on your situation and reminded you of truth. She expressed care and concern for you. That affected how you felt. What a wonderful way to help one another!

Of course this also means that we should invite people's encouragement. When we are feeling down, when we're struggling with anger, when we're aware of growing cold towards God, when we're wrestling with bitterness. Whatever it is, we should invite others to encourage us. We should ask to talk it through and be ready to be taught, rebuked or spurred on. We should hope to be given perspective and helped to feel rightly.

And it doesn't just have to be helping one another when we're down, sad or anxious. We can help one another to feel joyful, thankful and hopeful. Here's a psalm that would have been sung in Israel; people would have sung this to one another:

> Sing joyfully to the LORD, you righteous;
>> it is fitting for the upright to praise him.
> Praise the LORD with the harp;
>> make music to him on the ten-stringed lyre.

Sing to him a new song;
    play skilfully, and shout for joy.
(Psalm 33:1–3)

People are calling one another to praise God and rejoice in him. The very next verse begins with the important word: 'For . . .' There are reasons why we should do this: because God's Word is true, because God made us, because he blesses us and saves us. But the point is that they were telling one another to rejoice in God, and giving one another reasons to do so.

I need people to do this for me. Left to myself, I'll slide into self-centred despondency. I need people to get me to lift my head, look at God, see him again, and respond in praise and thanksgiving.

I know it's not easy, because it means being open, and that means making ourselves vulnerable. Saying what we are feeling, especially when those feelings are ugly and unpleasant, is exposing a very personal side of ourselves. But we do need help.

In fact, our feelings are often where we need help most. Feelings can be overwhelming and consuming. They can swamp us so that we don't know which way is up any more. But other people can bring perspective and proportion. Feelings can make us blind so that we don't quite realize how we're thinking and operating. But other people can shed fresh light, helping us to see ourselves rightly. Feelings can obscure the truth of the gospel, squeeze out everything else but what I'm feeling right now and make that the only

Others can remind me that God is good, that the gospel is good news, and that more things than my feelings are real.

reality. But others can remind me that God is good, that the gospel is good news, and that more things than my feelings are real.

Do you see how we can help one another? Do you see how we need one another?

Don't think you can grow in right and godly feeling on your own. You can't! If you think you can, then I'm sorry but you're proud and need to repent of that, and express your dependence on the Christian community.

Expressing feelings together

The community of the church is also where we express feelings together. The New Testament is full of commands and descriptions about how the church should live out life together, and that includes how we 'feel'. Here are some examples:

- 'Rejoice with those who rejoice; mourn with those who mourn' (Romans 12:15)
- 'Now that you have purified yourselves by obeying the truth so that you have sincere love for each other, love one another deeply, from the heart' (1 Peter 1:22)
- 'Be kind and compassionate to one another, forgiving each other, just as in Christ God forgave you' (Ephesians 4:32)
- 'Therefore, as God's chosen people, holy and dearly loved, clothe yourselves with compassion, kindness, humility, gentleness and patience. Bear with each other and forgive one another if any of you has a grievance against someone. Forgive as the Lord forgave you' (Colossians 3:12–13)

The life of the church is a life full of feeling! We are to identify with one another and feel for one another in life's ups and downs. We are to show love and compassion. When people do wrong things, we are to bear with them and forgive them.

God, in his wisdom, has put us together in churches to live this out. So church is a key part of the training ground for our emotions. Church life is not just about being taught, not about sitting in a meeting, but about relating to the rest of God's people in a way that is governed by his Word.

This isn't an optional part of church life. It's not that the real business of church is listening to sermons and doing evangelism, and then if we have time to relate to people, it's a bonus. The Bible passages above are describing everyday, normal Christian life.

When Paul says we have to bear with one another and forgive one another, what is he assuming? He's assuming that people will rub one another up the wrong way, do things that are annoying and do things that need forgiveness. He's assuming that we are relating to one another closely, closely enough to fall out, closely enough to need heart attitudes of patience and forbearance.

What is Paul assuming when he commands love, compassion and kindness? He's assuming that relationships are close enough for compassion to be shown. Paul's view of the Christian life is life in community. And this is all about attitudes and feelings in relationship.

Which is no more than what Jesus said. He said that people would know that we are his disciples if we loved one another (John 13:34–35). He said that we had to forgive one another from the heart (Matthew 18:35).

And this is precisely what we see in the life of Jesus. When we surveyed Jesus' emotions earlier, we saw how he felt towards the people around him. How he had compassion on those who were ill or facing tragedy. How he was concerned for those who were struggling. How he expressed love and patience and kindness to those around him.

And this is also what we see in the life of Paul (not that Paul's emotions were perfect, but he does set us a godly example in Scripture). He tells the Philippian Christians how he feels about them: 'God can testify how I long for all of you with the affection of Christ Jesus' (Philippians 1:8). He longs for them with a love that is like Jesus' love.

But elsewhere Paul expresses his anguish over the Corinthian church because they are doing badly: 'For I wrote to you out of great distress and anguish of heart and with many tears, not to grieve you but to let you know the depth of my love for you' (2 Corinthians 2:4). As he was writing his previous letter, tears were running down his cheeks. He felt for the church because he loved them so much. Similarly, Paul expresses his acute anxiety for the Galatian church because they are in danger of turning away from the true gospel (Galatians 4:19–20).

If we want to be like Christ or like Paul, these are the attitudes and feelings in which we need to grow and which we need *to express to one another in the life of the church*.

Differences in community

The church is also the place where we become aware of differences between us.

Dan played the drums, and Debbie sang in the music group. But they were like chalk and cheese. Dan was a computer programmer, very logical and technical. 'Awkward' was how some described him. Debbie was an art teacher, bubbly and extrovert. 'Gushy' was how some described her.

They played together in the music group, but all was not happy. When Debbie sang, she closed her eyes and raised her hands. She spoke afterwards about what a wonderful time of worship it had been. Dan watched, listened, said nothing, and felt second rate. At times though he comforted himself by thinking that Debbie was all froth. He occasionally reminded himself that she was very up and down – once she had had time out from singing because she was depressed. At least he was stable. Debbie meanwhile really wanted Dan to experience God more; she was worried for him because he seemed so unaffected by the worship. But on occasion she knew deep down she felt a bit superior.

Different people, different experiences. And that's just one (rather stereotypical) example. We differ in all manner of ways in what we feel and how we express our feelings. Some of us wear our hearts on our sleeves; others keep them well hidden. Some of us speak easily of what we feel for God or for people; others are much more reserved. Some of us shed a tear quite regularly; others can't remember the last time they cried.

But we're bound together in community. And that means we need two things. First we each need to be expressing right feelings to one another, and growing in our ability to do that. For some of us that feels very awkward, and we need to grow in learning how to express more. For others it's easy, and we may even need to learn more self-control, rather than letting whatever we're feeling pour out of us. Remember, we're not simply after emotional expression – we're after *godly* emotional expression.

Secondly, we need certain attitudes to help us live with these differences. Remember some of the sources of differences that we've covered: personality, background, memories, nationality? We need to say these differences are OK. We're not aiming at uniformity. We're aiming at reality for each one of us.

We need to be generous with one another, assuming the best rather than the worst. That's part of honouring one another above ourselves (Romans 12:10).

We need to avoid passing judgment on one another, and not cause one another to stumble (Romans 14:13).

We need to bear with one another, making allowance for different people to express themselves in different ways, rather than insisting on our way (Philippians 2:3–4).

And we need to do all of this, while spurring one another on to right feeling. We don't say necessarily that whatever someone feels, and however they express it, is OK. We still teach and encourage and rebuke one another.

It's tricky. But it can be done. And it makes for a wonderfully accepting community, and a wonderfully united community, and a community that is still concerned for my growth.

Emotions in community

Feelings are very personal things. But we are not to live them out by ourselves. Any individual, me-and-God type faith, where I'm happy as long as I feel OK, cannot be right.

We need one another to grow in godly feelings. We are to feel godly feelings for one another. We are to be united despite our different feelings. God made us to feel, and he made us to feel in community.

Questions for reflection

1. How do you think of church – more a meeting or a family? What might need to change?
2. Why do we need one another in growing in godly feelings? Can you give examples from your own experience?
3. What sorts of expression of feeling should exist in church life? Think of recent events in the lives of people in your church and ask, 'How should we feel about those?' How might those feelings be expressed?

4. What differences have you noticed between how you and others feel and express feelings? What issues has this raised?

5. What key attitudes do we need to have in our churches so that feelings are talked about, expressed and grown in?

9
feeling down

One of the most common feelings in the life of a Christian is feeling down. In fact this is true for everyone; it's just more complicated for Christians. It's more complicated because they feel like it shouldn't be like that. They should feel joy and happiness. Maybe they are told on a Sunday that they should praise God (as we've already seen), but still, their heart feels heavy and sad.

The common result? Feeling more down about being down. Along with feeling guilty for not feeling as they think they should.

The painful cry

We've seen that the Psalms are full of emotion, full of praise and joy, but also despair. Through the prism of the Psalms we see the painful cry of the heart:

How long, LORD? Will you forget me forever?
How long will you hide your face from me?

How long must I wrestle with my thoughts
　and day after day have sorrow in my heart?
　How long will my enemy triumph over me?
(Psalm 13:1–2)

My heart is in anguish within me;
　the terrors of death have fallen on me.
Fear and trembling have beset me;
　horror has overwhelmed me.
(Psalm 55:4–5)

I am overwhelmed with troubles
　and my life draws near to death.
I am counted among those who go down to the pit;
　I am like one without strength.
(Psalm 88:3–4)

The Bible is unembarrassed about these feelings. The psalmist says it how it is. God believes in emotional honesty. And so if we are feeling some of these 'negative' emotions – sorrow, anguish, fear, trouble – we should feel free to say so.

Unfortunately, that has not always been the case in history. Christians have often felt like they should suppress such feelings, and certainly not talk about them. The church has sometimes been the last place where we would be honest like this. Of course that varies from church to church, but many people still feel reluctant. There's an important role here for leaders and small-group leaders: to encourage and model emotional honesty.

Notice that these emotions are expressed in psalms which were publicly known, and probably used in congregational songs and prayers. Theologian Carl Trueman wrote an editorial called: 'What Can Miserable Christians Sing?'[1] His point? That the Psalms are full of these painful cries of the heart, whereas songs today tend only to speak of joy. But that only adds to the feeling of burden on people and buys into the idea that Christians should be happy all the time. (I'm pleased to say that I've noticed a few more songs recently that have expressed a wider range of feelings.)

Lastly, we see that there are times when it is right to feel down (which is what is assumed from the points above). In each of the psalms I've quoted there's a very good reason to feel down, to feel distressed, to feel overwhelmed. We saw this earlier when looking at Jesus – and there are lots of sad things in life over which we should feel sad. There are things that are distressing, and we should feel distress – indeed it would be wrong and inhuman not to do so.

Spotting the difference

This means we need to learn to spot the difference between feeling down for good and bad reasons. Now that's not always easy, but we've got to have a go. Here is a key place for reflection. We saw earlier how our emotions give us a window into our hearts. We obviously don't want to encourage unhelpful introspection, but it can be really helpful to ask where our feelings are coming from.

Counsellor David Powlison writes, 'Wise living involves alertness to experience and emotion.' But he also warns: 'The goal of such awareness is not introspective self-preoccupation. Such awareness is rather a matter of integrity and honesty.'[2] In other words, we want to be aware of our feelings so that we're being honest about what is happening in our lives and in our hearts. We want to examine why we're feeling something so that we avoid a 'split personality', where we say one thing but feel another.

So we might feel overwhelmed and stressed out. My wife felt like that recently. The reason? It was simply a time when there was too much on, too much to think about, too much to do. What she needed was a return to normal life.

Why am I stressed?

- Is it because I'm not trusting God's sovereign care, not casting my anxieties on him or turning to him in prayer (1 Peter 5:7; Philippians 4:6–7)?
- Is it because I am trying to do too much? If so, why?
- Is it to prove myself, or to make a success of my career?
- Is it because I refuse the help of others, not wanting to be dependent on people or to be seen to be weak, which could be plain old sinful pride?

Or take anger. Why am I feeling angry? OK, it could be that there's something I really should be angry about – my anger is appropriate. But behind anger often lies frustration. That might be frustration at not getting my own way, or frustration with sin, or frustration with other people, or frustration that I'm not in control. And that frustration shows itself in angry outbursts.

Of course we can, and should, ask the same question about positive emotions. Why am I feeling happy and satisfied? Is it because I am enjoying God and living for him, enjoying his blessings in family, church, work and friends? If so, great! What a fantastic thing! God means us to be happy; he's not against it. But I know, as someone who gives talks, that I can be happy because I've been asked to speak at a conference and I think this reflects well on me. Not so good. We can be satisfied because we've impressed someone or because we think we look good today.

So first, be honest about your emotions. Secondly, try to spot the difference between feeling down for good and bad reasons.

And here is a third piece of advice: speak truth to yourself.

Speaking truth to yourself

Psalms 42 and 43 are well known as psalms about being 'down'. These two are put together because of the repeated refrain that runs through both of them:

> Why, my soul, are you downcast?
>> Why so disturbed within me?
> Put your hope in God,
>> for I will yet praise him,
>> my Saviour and my God.
> (Psalm 42:5)

Here is someone being honest. And in the rest of the psalm he speaks about how rubbish life is. He says, 'My tears have been my food day and night' (42:3). He says God has forgotten him. He is totally honest.

But he also *talks* to himself about how he feels. We should be honest, but that doesn't mean we stay there. What we see in Psalms 42–43 is someone wrestling with his own feelings and speaking truth to himself:

> These things I remember
>> as I pour out my soul:
> how I used to go to the house of God
>> under the protection of the Mighty One
> with shouts of joy and praise
>> among the festive throng.
> (Psalm 42:4)

He remembers how he used to go to the temple and praise God, how he used to be filled with joy. I don't think he is simply saying, 'It used to be better.' He is reminding himself of truth about God:

My soul is downcast within me;
    therefore I will remember you
from the land of the Jordan,
    the heights of Hermon – from Mount Mizar.
(Psalm 42:6)

He is far away from the temple in Jerusalem in the land of the Jordan (which is where the mountains of Hermon are). But he focuses his attention and simply remembers God:

By day the LORD directs his love,
    at night his song is with me –
    a prayer to the God of my life.
(Psalm 42:8)

He remembers that, despite how he feels, God is the one who has promised to love him. He uses the special covenant name for God here ('the LORD') which was about God's faithfulness to his covenant promises; and he uses the word for 'covenant-love', the love which God has promised. And he says that the LORD directs, or commands, that love. God tells his love where to go. He is remembering God as the one who has committed himself to love us.

So he talks to himself, questions himself, reminds himself of truth. And then in that repeated refrain the psalmist tells himself (three times) what to do: to put his hope in God and to look forward to praising him again. It's like me saying,

'Come on, Graham, trust God, he is good; look to him, you will rejoice in him again.'

The famous pastor Dr Martyn Lloyd-Jones helpfully commented on this:

> I say that we must talk to ourselves instead of allowing 'ourselves' to talk to us! . . . Have you realized that most of your unhappiness in life is due to the fact that you are listening to yourself instead of talking to yourself? . . . You have to take yourself in hand, you have to address yourself, preach to yourself, question yourself.[3]

Here's how to respond to being down. Talk truth to yourself and tell yourself what to do. This is very countercultural, because we are so often told to listen to our feelings. OK, there is some point in that, in being aware of how we feel, but we must not be dictated to by our feelings. Instead we must speak truth to ourselves.

Here's how to respond to being down. Talk truth to yourself and tell yourself what to do.

Now that doesn't mean we won't still feel down. We may in fact continue to feel sad because we're in a sad situation. But within our sadness we will speak truth to ourselves to remind ourselves that this isn't all of reality: God is still good; God is still loving. We will encourage ourselves to put our hope in God within our sadness and look forward to the time when we'll praise him again.

It might be we have no good reason to feel very down. In which case we speak truth to ourselves to talk ourselves out of it. We tell ourselves off – you've got no reason to be sad. We tell ourselves how good God is and to rejoice in him.

This is what we see in the Psalms all the time: honest sadness, distress and despondency expressed. And then truth is spoken. Encouragement is given. People spur themselves on.

Praying

We also see people turning to God in prayer. They are not just honest about how they feel, but honest *to God* about how they feel. They don't just remind themselves of truth; they remind themselves *in prayer* of that truth. And they also, in a simple and straightforward way, ask God to change their situation.

In Psalm 43 the psalmist prays that God would 'rescue' him. He goes on:

> Send me your light and your faithful care,
> > let them lead me;
> let them bring me to your holy mountain,
> > to the place where you dwell.
> (Psalm 43:3)

He's asking God to bring him to Jerusalem, where the temple is. He's asking for a chance to be in God's presence. He goes on:

> Then I will go to the altar of God,
> > to God, my joy and my delight.
> I will praise you with the lyre,
> > O God, my God.
> (Psalm 43:4)

He's asking God to bring him to the point where he will praise him again in the temple. But notice that, as he does so, he reminds himself that God is his 'joy and delight'. Here is a wonderful mix of honesty, request and reminder, jumbled together in prayer.

Do we pray like this?

We can so easily feel victims of our emotions and simply allow them to wash over us. If we do pray about how we feel, we simply ask God to help us feel happier, or to change our situation so that we feel happier. Here we see someone taking his situation and feelings to God and talking it through. Arguing with himself and arguing with God.

When we feel down, sad, grieving and despairing, we need to turn to God in real, honest, wrestling prayer. Ask him to give you joy in him, but also ask him why he hasn't done so now. Tell him how you feel, but also tell him that you love him. Call on him to change your situation, but also call on him to change your heart.

Getting on with living

Jane's story

Jane was feeling down. It was the summer holidays after her second year at university. She'd not done well in her end-of-term exams, and her holiday plans with a friend had collapsed. (The friend had money trouble.)

The result was that Jane was hanging around at home not doing very much. She'd taken to staying up pretty late, spending time on the web (mainly Facebook and eBay). She spent quite a few hours watching daytime TV. She mulled on her poor exam marks – why had she been so stupid? She repeated her frustrations about her friend over and over – she'd known how much the holiday cost, so what had been so difficult?

Jane mainly felt flat and depressed. She'd got to the stage of not even responding to calls and texts from friends.

What would you suggest Jane does?

Reflecting on why she feels down and speaking truth to herself would be a good start. This should make a huge difference.

But Jane would also feel better if she got out more. It would be good to get on with arranging another holiday or to visit a friend, rather than lamenting the holiday she'd missed out on. She would also feel better if she got some more sleep and did something constructive and productive with her days.

Of course if she did these things and didn't change her thinking or her heart, then any feeling better would be fairly superficial. But what we do does affect how we feel. This can work in different ways:

Our living can reinforce how we're feeling. If I feel down and mope around all day, I'll only feel more down. It all has to do with what I focus on. If I mope around, I'll focus on whatever I think is wrong: I'll play over and over whatever is getting me down. Whereas if I decide to get on with life and do something positive, I'll redirect my thinking.

Our living can stimulate new feelings. Getting on with something productive means I will start to feel more positive. Jane might arrange to go out with a friend, even when she doesn't feel like it, and in doing so she will probably start to feel differently. Acting changes our focus, brings a new experience and stimulates new feelings.

We must remember that we are connected, whole people. Our acting, feeling and thinking all combine, and so when we're feeling down, we need to do our best to get on with living life rather than curling up into a ball (especially if it's a self-pitying ball).

Getting on with obeying

We can even go a step further. It's not simply that getting on with living can change our feelings; obeying God is sometimes needed before we actually feel anything. In John 15, Jesus is talking about how we should remain in him, that is, stay close and obey him. And he goes on: 'If you keep my commands, you will remain in my love, just as I have kept my Father's commands and remain in his love. I have told you this so that my joy may be in you and that your joy may be complete' (John 15:10–11).

Keeping Jesus' commands results in his joy being in us and our joy being complete. Jesus rejoiced to obey God, rejoicing in a life lived for his Father's glory and a faithful completion of the work he had been sent to do. And now he says we can have his joy in us, and that means our joy being complete or full.

But to gain that joy, we have to live in obedience, remaining in Jesus' love. We need to be committed to God and live out our trust in him before we will enjoy the reality of our relationship with him. For example, if we are to know God's peace, we actually have to trust his promises and live them out. If we keep on living as if those promises weren't true, then we won't know that peace.

This is why ongoing sin usually robs the Christian of his joy and brings him down. I remember talking to a wise pastor many years ago. We were talking about assurance in the Christian life and how to help someone who felt like God was far away. One of the first things he said was to ask the person if there was any sin unrepented of in their life! It didn't strike me as very caring at the time. But it was wise, and this is why: we remain in Jesus' love and know his joy by obeying him.

Now that doesn't mean perfection. But it does mean a life orientated to Jesus, staying loyal to him. It means that, as we become aware of sin, there is confession and repentance, rather than resistance and denial. It means that, as John says in his letter, we walk in the light, not in the darkness (1 John 1:6–7).

Psalm 32 talks in graphic terms of how David felt when he refused to acknowledge and confess his sin:

> When I kept silent,
> my bones wasted away
> through my groaning all day long.
> For day and night
> your hand was heavy on me;
> my strength was sapped
> as in the heat of summer.
> (Psalm 32:3–4)

Resisting God resulted in groaning and a feeling of wasting away. It doesn't always feel like that of course, for some people celebrate their sin and feel good in it. But the true Christian will have some element of guilt and a loss of joy and peace.

Wonderfully, the psalm goes on:

> Then I acknowledged my sin to you
> and did not cover up my iniquity.
> I said, 'I will confess
> my transgressions to the LORD.'
> And you forgave
> the guilt of my sin.
> (Psalm 32:5)

Acknowledgment and confession lead to forgiveness and restoration. And this brings us back to knowing God's love and joy. In Psalm 51 David confesses his sins of adultery and murder. Having asked for forgiveness, he says, 'Restore to me the joy of your salvation' (Psalm 51:12). We can lose the joy of salvation through resisting God, but wonderfully we can regain it through confession.

We can lose the joy of salvation through resisting God, but wonderfully we can regain it through confession.

This is why Psalm 32 began with a cry of joy:

Blessed is the one
    whose transgressions are forgiven,
    whose sins are covered.
Blessed is the one
    whose sin the LORD does not count against them
    and in whose spirit is no deceit.
(Psalm 32:1–2)

When we stop covering up our sin, God covers it up for us. And there is a wonderful joy in forgiveness and in the knowledge that our sin has been taken away. But to have that blessing, we have to be those who have no 'deceit' in us. We have to be living honestly before God, trying to follow him.

Depression
Thinking about feeling down raises the thorny issue of depression. It's difficult because it's complicated, difficult because it's so personal and difficult because it's so painful.

But we do need to say it: Christians get depressed. In one church of about a hundred adults that I attended I knew of about five who had suffered from very serious bouts of depression, and another fifteen who had had milder forms. That's about one in five.

Of all our painful feelings, depression brings some of the worst. A feeling that God has turned his back on us. That there's no point in praying because God is not listening. That there's no point living at all. These are awful things, but we must acknowledge that Christians can and do experience such feelings.

Counsellor Ed Welch relays some of the different descriptions of depression: 'The images are dark and evocative. Desperately alone, doom, black holes, deep wells, emptiness.' Some individuals lie awake at night with 'anguish, fears and a torrent of pain'. At other times it can be a 'steady drizzle of fear, pain, guilt, panic, deadness and fatigue'. Of other people he says,

> Instead of a bottomless abyss and howling in the brain, life is flat, grey and cold. Nothing holds any interest. You are a barely walking zombie. Everything is drab, lifeless and tired. Why work? Why get out of bed? Why do anything? Why commit suicide? Nothing seems to matter.[4]

If you have never suffered from it, depression can be hard to understand. It is also very isolating.

Depression can come from a variety of sources, and it often arises because of several things combining – rarely because of one single cause. It can be a reaction to life situations, especially loss of some kind: loss of a relative, loss of a job, loss of a role. It can even be the loss of something I don't yet have but which was a possibility – loss of a potential future.

But it can also just arise seemingly by itself with no clearly linked external cause.

It can come from certain physiological conditions, one of the most common being post-natal depression which involves hormonal changes after childbirth – although that's not the only factor. It does seem likely that some people are more disposed towards depression than others and that this might be something to do with their physiological make-up.

Depression can arise from certain backgrounds. Or perhaps more accurately, certain backgrounds and upbringing come into play and add to its effect.

I am no expert on depression and we don't have space in this book to say much about it, but here are a few observations to help us. (For more, turn to the recommended further reading section at the end of the book.)

Seeking help
Depression isolates people. They have no motivation or desire to interact, so they withdraw instead. One of the first things you should do if you are aware of becoming depressed is to seek help, and do so early. Talk to a good Christian friend, your small-group leader or a staff worker at your church. If you think someone you know is depressed, try to talk to them yourself and encourage them to seek help. There's no need for drama; just start talking.

Counselling
Depression flows from the sources above, and a key element of combatting depression is understanding why it is there in the first place. I need to know why I feel as I do, and then think through how to respond. The most helpful thing in all of this is talking with someone else. It could be the person mentioned

above or it could be someone with specific training in coun-
selling. The choice depends on a lot of factors.

Medical help

Medical help can also be perfectly appropriate. Anti-depressants
may provide stability to allow the sufferer to work through
the issues. Medication shouldn't simply be used to cover
over the issue and not address what is going on, but it can
really help in getting through the severe stages. It may have a
place more long term for some people as well. But it means
you need to talk to your doctor, and to your pastor or a
Christian counsellor.

'Normal' help

Of course there are normal things we can do to help ourselves
when we're depressed, and we've covered some of the most
important ones already. We should be reflecting on why we're
down, seeking to speak truth to ourselves, praying for God's
help, and looking to get on with living life and obeying God.
We should watch normal things like our diet, sleep and
exercise which can play into how we feel. Being depressed is
not a special state where those 'normal' responses don't apply
any more.

The difference with depression can be that we are feeling
so low that we aren't able to do the normal stuff. We can go
through times when we feel we can't pray or speak truth
to ourselves. These are times when the help above comes
into play.

Pressing on

We should not be surprised by times of feeling down, and
even depression. The nineteenth-century preacher Charles
Spurgeon gave a talk to ministers, advising them not to be

surprised: 'Fits of depression come over the most of us. Cheerful as we may be, we must at intervals be cast down. The strong are not always vigorous, the wise not always ready, the brave not always courageous, and the joyous not always happy.'

If we're feeling down, we are in good company with godly people in the Bible and down through the centuries ever since. What we need to do is to look to their example of pressing on in trusting God even when the path is dark.

Spurgeon says: 'Put no trust in frames and feelings. Care more for a grain of faith than a ton of excitement. Trust in God alone.'[5]

Questions for reflection

1. Do you feel able to be honest about feeling down? Why or why not?
2. Why is it so important to recognize the 'painful cry' of Christians?
3. How can we tell the difference between feeling down for good and bad reasons?
4. How can you speak the truth to yourself when feeling down? Have you experienced this? What difference did it make?
5. What experience of depression do you have – for yourself or others? What helped or hindered in that situation?

10
knowing what to expect and facing the future

I hope you've been encouraged to be positive about emotion. I hope you are now trying to grow in good and godly emotions. I hope you will rejoice in God, know his peace and overflow with thanksgiving. I hope too you're also learning to cry over sin and injustice. I hope you've seen how God made us to live life in colour.

There's one last perspective and that's dealing with the ups and downs of our emotional life. There will be wonderful days of sunshine and gloomy days of rain. And between the two, just plain ordinary days.

Expect mixed feelings

Many people think that the Christian emotional life is supposed to be a never-ending sunny smile. We know that the reality is very different. But it's such a common stereotype that it's worth mentioning again.

We hope to be those who rejoice in God and know his

peace. But that's not all. In other words, *we should expect mixed feelings*.

We saw Jesus rejoicing *and* feeling anguish. We saw the psalmist shouting praise, and crying in pain. The apostle Paul tells us to rejoice always (Philippians 4:4), and says that he is full of joy (e.g. Philippians 1:4). But in the same book he speaks about a friend who was ill and almost died, and Paul says he faced 'sorrow upon sorrow' (Philippians 2:27). He would have been devastated by that friend's death.

Again, Paul tells us not to be anxious about anything but to pray to God and know his peace (Philippians 4:6–7). But in the same letter he speaks about his anxiety over the friend who was ill (Philippians 2:28). Clearly there is such a thing as untrusting, ungodly anxiety. But there is also such a thing as appropriate concern! If one of my children is seriously ill, I should be worried. If my spouse dies, I should feel great sorrow. It would be strange not to! (And very inhuman too.)

Romans 8 speaks about how the whole world is groaning as in childbirth, and that we are groaning too:

> We know that the whole creation has been groaning as in the pains of childbirth right up to the present time. Not only so, but we ourselves, who have the firstfruits of the Spirit, groan inwardly as we wait eagerly for our adoption to sonship, the redemption of our bodies.
> (Romans 8:22–23)

We groan over all that is wrong with the world. We feel pain and concern; we shed tears and sigh; and we long for the bright glorious day to come when the groaning will be over.

This means we must beware of the caricature of the happy, smiling Christian. To be honest, I don't trust a happy, smiling Christian – something is usually being covered up. We will feel a whole variety of emotions, including 'negative' ones. Those negative emotions, felt for good reason, are right, normal, expected and godly.

So we should expect a mixed emotional life. Not a bit of up and a bit of down, which means we end up somewhere in the middle. But genuine highs and genuine lows. That's what we saw in Jesus, in the Psalms and in the apostle Paul.

We feel pain and concern; we shed tears and sigh; and we long for the bright glorious day to come when the groaning will be over.

Peter begins his first letter by speaking about the wonders of salvation and the hope we have for the future, and then speaks about our mixed emotions: 'In all this you greatly rejoice, though now for a little while you may have had to suffer grief in all kinds of trials' (1 Peter 1:6).

We rejoice now. And we suffer grief now. Both are true at the same time.

We can't live on a high

Let me introduce you to Sally – I say she's called Sally but I actually have no idea what her name was. She is someone who met Jesus in Luke 7.

Jesus is visiting a Pharisee called Simon. But while he's there, Sally turns up:

> A woman in that town who lived a sinful life learned that Jesus was eating at the Pharisee's house, so she came there with an alabaster jar of perfume. As she stood behind him at his feet weeping, she began to wet his feet with her tears. Then she wiped them with her hair, kissed them and poured perfume on them. (Luke 7:37–38)

Now I think Sally had met Jesus before – because of something Jesus says later on. But now she hears that Jesus is in town, and so she heads off with her jar of perfume. She is planning on showing her respect and love for Jesus by anointing him with it. It's the ancient equivalent of calling round with an expensive gift of some kind. But when she gets there, it seems she is overcome with emotion.

She is behind Jesus, standing by his feet. (Jesus would have been reclining to eat.) And as she stands there, she starts weeping. It seems like the tears are flowing pretty freely, because there are enough for Jesus' feet to be wet with them. And then, with nothing else available, she wipes his feet with her hair, and kisses them. And then pours the perfume on them.

It is an amazing moment of emotional outpouring.

Jesus explains later what has happened. He says it is all an expression of Sally's love for him: 'Therefore, I tell you, her many sins have been forgiven – as her great love has shown' (Luke 7:47).

Jesus sees this great affection as a display of Sally's love, because she has been forgiven. Her love hasn't earned her forgiveness; it is how she feels having been forgiven.

This is why I think Sally had met Jesus already, or at least had heard him speak and responded. Because Jesus is saying that she came with her expensive bottle of perfume to say thank you, to express her love. And her love is so great that, when she arrived, it resulted in this great outpouring of emotion and tears and kisses.

There will be times when we may feel similar to Sally. We will be full of great love for Jesus. It will be because we are aware of our sin, its ugliness and nastiness, and aware of God's mercy, its freedom and graciousness. We'll be aware of Jesus' forgiveness, its fullness and completeness. That might not mean tears, but whatever our personality is, we will feel great love for him.

But what do you think Sally felt the next morning? Or the next week? Or the next month? Or the next year? I don't think she went around perpetually weeping. The thing about that kind of intense emotion is that it can't actually last long. Whatever it is that has struck us deeply soon becomes more familiar. Or whatever we are sad about eases off. We are simply not built to live with an ongoing intense emotional outpouring.

I think for Sally the intensity of emotion that day would have given way to a quiet reassurance and a peaceful gratitude. Maybe at moments as she reflected on her life and thought about her forgiveness, a tear would have come to her eye again. But she would have dried her eyes and pressed on with life.

So here's the point. We can't live on an emotional high. We may at times feel great love, great joy or great peace. And those feelings may be intense. But we don't live with them from that point on. We feel those things because of how focused we are on certain truths about Jesus at that point, and how those truths strike us. But we can't live life always focused like that. There is work to be done; there are children to be cared for, people to talk to. Life is not to be lived kneeling before God and crying.

Life is not to be lived feeling overwhelmed with emotion.

So as well as mixed emotions, we must also expect a variation in emotion. We should hope and expect that, as we focus on God, as we bring his grace to mind, as we are taught about him, as we sing of him, we will feel more. That's great. But at other times we will feel less, and our attention will be elsewhere. That's not to say we no longer have any joy, or peace or gratitude. But we don't have the same degree of intensity. We can't. And that's OK.

Feeling and seeing

We must also deal with the fact that we will not feel all that we
think we should, or all that we want to.

Matt's story

I had become really worried about what I felt for God. It came
from a book I was reading on how we should delight in God
above everything else. The author spoke about all our desires
being met in God, our having complete satisfaction and joy
in him. He warned about rejoicing in anything else apart
from God.

It made me really anxious, and it really troubled me.

I could see that some of the challenge was good. I had felt
more joy in what I had owned and what I had achieved than in
God, and I was sorry about that. But I kept questioning myself:
'Why don't I feel more?'

I began to wonder if I was really a Christian at all.

Some Christians suggest that, if we really understand God,
really grasp what he's done, then our joy will be overwhelming. But there's one issue I worry that they might be missing:
Paul says, 'We live by faith, not by sight' (2 Corinthians 5:7).

All the realities of the gospel are realities, but we can't see
them yet. We can't see God and his goodness. We can't
see our forgiveness and righteousness in Christ. We can't see
our adoption as children of God. We can't see our future
inheritance. We know God has been incredibly good to us,
and so we should be grateful, but we can't see it. We know
salvation is a wonderful thing that we should rejoice in, but
we can't actually see it.

We live by faith.

Living by faith doesn't mean just deciding to believe that the promises of the gospel are true. We have faith in them, taking God at his word, and we have good reason to do so.

I might promise my children a treat when we get home: ice cream in front of the TV (yes, that's a treat in our house). And they look forward to it. They might even rejoice in the idea of it! But they're living by faith, not by sight, taking me at my word. They haven't got the treat yet, nor can they see it. That doesn't mean it's wrong to hope and rejoice. But it does make it different from the moment when they're holding the bowl of ice cream in their hands.

All the realities of the gospel are realities, but we can't see them yet.

Our emotions tend to be raised by our five senses: things we can see, touch, taste, feel and smell. Our senses affect us more directly than unseen things and raise an emotional response. This is why I can be so affected by a film – I hear the dialogue, I see the expressions, I'm aware of the music. But here's the point: we can't use those senses on the truths of the gospel.

This is not to say we can't be affected by those truths we can't see. God's Spirit makes them real to us, bringing us an awareness of sin, confidence in the gospel, knowledge of God's love. These things are real to us, but they are real by faith.

This is why it is easier to feel rightly for concrete situations around us than for spiritual truths. We can see and touch the physical situation. We can't see or touch the spiritual reality.

This is why we will always have to work at reminding

ourselves of truths about God and feeling rightly in the light of them. When we actually see something, the feelings usually flow by themselves.

If you stand in front of the Grand Canyon, you will feel enormous awe and wonder. But you will have to *remind* yourself of God's majesty and splendour in order to feel awe about him.

If you are treated kindly by someone when you don't deserve it, you will feel gratitude. But you will have to remind yourself of God's kindness to feel grateful to him.

If you look at a beautiful jewel, painting, car or house (whatever it is for you), you will easily feel a great desire for it. But you will have to remind yourself of God's beauty in order to desire him above all else.

This explains why right feelings are a battle.

This explains why we'll easily feel more about the things of this world which we can see and touch.

This explains why I easily feel more watching a film than reading my Bible.

This means that, when we see God clearly, face to face, we'll have no problem with our feelings. When we see him as he is, the right feelings will flow.

This means there is an ongoing need to remind ourselves of God's truth. We see the truth about God as we read his Word and hear it taught. We sense the truth of the gospel as we remind one another of it. We touch the wonder of the gospel as we celebrate it in song. We need constant reminders of what's true, what's real.

Expect the normal Christian life

Growth in godly feelings is part of the normal Christian life, part of becoming more like Jesus. Here are some things to help us with our expectations.

Growth in godly feelings will be gradual

We don't become like Jesus overnight. Shame I know, but that's how God is doing it. He's changing us from one degree of glory to another, not doing one-stop shopping (2 Corinthians 3:18). Of course we feel some things rightly from the very start of our Christian life. We might feel great joy in salvation or great love for our neighbour. Wonderful!

But of course the next month we might not. That's partly because of all the reasons mentioned above. But it's also because it takes time for our hearts to change. Heart change is slow and gradual. And heart change is what lies behind emotion change.

We will fail and need forgiveness

It might sound obvious, but it needs saying. We are going to continue to mess up. We fail and sin in every part of life, and that will be true for our emotions too. We'll feel angry when we shouldn't, feel sad over something that isn't worth it, rejoice in something selfish. And we'll continue to sin for the rest of our lives.

But we are to keep on battling with sin. Keep on praying for God's help. And we're to keep on asking for forgiveness. There is ongoing forgiveness from God for our sinful emotions just as for every other area of sin.

We will do battle until we die

Isaac Watts, the hymn writer, said, 'The grave is the only burying place of unruly affections.'[1]

We will keep on battling with feeling rightly until our death. The battles might change. As we get older, we might have to battle with nostalgia or bitterness rather than envy or greed. But whatever may change in the battle, the battle will continue.

We are to look forward

But we look forward to the day when God's work of re-creating us is complete. We look forward to the new creation when we will only and always feel rightly. And when God re-creates everything as it should be, there will be nothing to cause us to cry or to mourn. There will be nothing to make us angry or sad. We will be with God.

And that will feel wonderful.

Questions for reflection

1. Why should we expect mixed feelings in the Christian life?
2. How might we go astray if we don't appreciate this?
3. What variation in feelings do you think we should expect over time?
4. What difference does it make to our emotions that we live by faith and not by sight?
5. How is part of growth in godly feelings simply part of the normal Christian life?
6. What difference does it make to understand all this?

appendix
a note to those in
Christian ministry

I want to say something to those of you in Christian ministry. By that I mean anyone involved in teaching the Bible to others and helping them grow in their discipleship. That might mean you are on the staff of a church, that you lead a small group, are involved in youth ministry or that you meet up one to one with a younger Christian.

If that's you, then I expect you've already thought of the many implications of what we've covered in this book. I just want to highlight a few.

1. Application to our own life

It's very easy for those involved in ministry to grow in knowledge alone, and for it to remain unapplied to our lives and to our hearts. So we need to apply these truths about feelings to ourselves. This is essential if we are to avoid a distant, professional approach where we know the truth but keep it from affecting us personally.

The dangers of that are many, but one of the most common is that we cease to rejoice in the gospel ourselves and the work of ministry becomes instead our source of joy. Broughton Knox was very influential in training ministers. He wrote a short essay on joy in Christian ministry, reflecting on Jesus' words to his disciples after their successful preaching and healing tour: 'However, do not rejoice that the spirits submit to you, but rejoice that your names are written in heaven' (Luke 10:20). Knox asks ministers whether they are being obedient to that charge, whether they are reflecting on God's goodness to us in salvation and rejoicing in it. He says,

> There is joy in ministry and we should all taste it. But there is greater, more serene joy in the relationship with God on which this ministry is based. So, as we minister in his name, we should be obedient to the command of our Lord and rejoice greatly, rejoice continually, that our names, with the names of our fellow Christians, the fellow members of our congregation, are written by God in heaven.[1]

When we know that greater joy, it gives a foundation to all we do and means that we keep going, and even rejoicing, when ministry is hard.

Application to ourselves is also true for our attitudes to other people. We should love our congregations; we should be anxious about those we fear are rejecting the gospel; we should be upset over sin or division; we should be glad and thankful over sacrificial giving or care in the church. We should feel these things, not just know in our heads that they are good or right.

But for these attitudes to be present we need to go to work on our own hearts, not just teach other people about their hearts.

2. Ministry to the whole person

We should not be content to fill people's heads with knowledge, or to fill their lives with obedience; we also want to change how people feel.

That means we need to help people understand themselves – thinking, feeling and acting – and help them understand the connections. If we don't, then they won't know how these things tie together.

We'll communicate this in at least two ways. First, we can do it implicitly: we'll speak about the truth of God and then we'll make an application to thanksgiving or contentment. And the very fact that we move from one to the other will implicitly show what we think the connections are. (People I know in ministry are all doing this already; I just want to suggest that we make some of the connections more obvious.)

Secondly, we may want to teach explicitly about this. That might be in a specific pastoral situation where someone is struggling with how they feel. Or it can be as part of the public teaching of the church, in small groups or seminars. As I have taught on this topic, one of the most common responses has been, 'I've never heard anything on this before.' We do need to address it.

We need both to encourage and warn people about this. Encourage the connected knowledge, feeling and action we've described. Encourage joy in God and love for one another. Encourage speaking truth to ourselves and warming our hearts with the truth of the gospel.

We want to warn against disconnection and against misuse of the emotions. Warn against knowledge that just remains knowledge, or action that is unthinking or wrongly motivated. Warn against the inappropriate seeking of emotional experience. Warn against emotion that is not grounded in knowledge, or people following emotion, or using it as the basis for their belief or action.

We must remember what we said about the culture of our day. It leads people to think with their feelings, decide with their feelings and live by their feelings. So it can lead people into disobedience, or into seeking experience for its own sake. This undermines true discipleship all around us. Our response is not to deny feelings, but to teach people their right place.

We will also want to show people how there is both commonality and individuality between us. We need to teach on the reasons for variation in emotions in how they are felt and expressed. In churches we want to encourage generosity and humility in this area, and warn against a judgmental attitude over emotions.

This will mean above all that we spend time trying to help people cultivate right hearts rather than just right knowledge. Jonathan Edwards spoke of this aim in preaching, but it applies to all of ministry. He said that we should not want to give people only a good doctrinal understanding, but to impress truth on people's hearts and affections. He said one way we do this is 'by often bringing the great things of religion to their remembrance, and setting them before them in their proper colours, though they know them, and have been fully instructed in them already'.[2]

So Edwards saw a key place for frequent reminders of what was already understood, by a presentation of the truth in its 'proper colours'. I pray that as I teach, talk and care for people, I will regularly present the gospel in its proper colours.

3. Evaluating our own ministry

It can be helpful to ask ourselves questions about what we think Christian maturity looks like, and then how that shows itself in our ministry. Imagine someone who focuses on 'thinking' and 'knowledge' as key features of maturity. Picture what their ministry would look like. For example:

- How would they spend time with people?
- What sort of questions would they ask?
- What would they look for in people?
- Who would they trust with responsibilities in the church?
- What sort of meetings would they organize?

And then do the same with someone who is focused on 'feelings', and someone who is focused on 'actions'. Focusing on a different picture of Christian maturity results in different shapes and priorities to ministry, and certain tell-tale signs appear. What we should want of course is a connected and rounded view of Christian maturity, involving our thinking, feeling and actions.

Ask yourself: 'What does my ministry look like?' 'What view of maturity does it reflect?' 'What would I want to change?'

4. Our preaching

Not everyone involved in ministry preaches sermons, but many do so and here are a few thoughts.

We should want our preaching to combine all three elements of knowledge, action and feeling. It's worth recognizing that the proportions of those in any one sermon will, and should, vary depending on the passage or topic we're talking about. Some passages are heavy in knowledge, for example sections of Romans. Some are heavy in emotion, for example the Psalms. Some passages focus around action such as the sections at the end of the letters, urging people to live out their faith.

I think our sermons should look for, and follow, the focus and balance of each passage. That might sound obvious, but I suggest we need to do that deliberately because, left to ourselves, we will easily slide towards our default position, where we mainly pick up on the element we are most attracted to.

For example in preaching the first half of Ephesians 1, we could easily find ourselves deep in knowledge about predestination, adoption, forgiveness, redemption, grace and so on. Which is all there in the passage and does need to be talked about. But we could forget that the framing of that whole passage is 'praise'. And so if by the end of my sermon, I haven't led people to marvel at God and to praise him, then I haven't preached it very well at all.

So as we approach a passage and prepare a sermon, it's worth asking ourselves from the passage: 'What should I know?' 'What should I do?' 'What should I feel?' And then ask which of these is the main focus.

There are also implications for how we structure sermons, which is often seen in the headings we use. I believe there are many and various ways of structuring sermons, and it is often driven by the passage concerned. But one spectrum worth thinking about is these three areas: knowledge, feeling and action.

This is best seen in an example. Philippians 1 includes Paul's comments on the partnership of the Philippians in the work of the gospel. He says: 'In all my prayers for all of you, I always pray with joy because of your partnership in the gospel from the first day until now' (Philippians 1:4–5).

Just think, 'How could I structure a sermon point from that section?' I could have a heading that says:

• The importance of Christian partnership

That focuses on what I should *think* about partnership – that it is important. I would talk about what it involves and why Paul thinks it is important, and then I would move to apply it to us and urge us to be involved in partnership.

Or I could have a heading that says:

• Give yourself to partnership

This now focuses on the application towards *action*. I would of course explain why Paul thinks it is important and what it involves, but my heading tells us to do something. The result is that the feel of this point in the sermon will be more applied, angled towards giving ourselves through our money, time or effort.

Or I could have a heading that says:

• Rejoice in partnership in the gospel

This is now focused on my *feelings*. Again I would explain what is happening in the passage, but I'm angling at how we should feel about something, how we should value it. That will lead on to how feeling that way will show itself in practice, in our giving and our prayer.

It is actually the last of these that picks up on the actual feelings expressed in the passage, because Paul says he prays with joy because of the Philippians' partnership in the gospel.

The best structure will vary enormously according to the passage, but asking which of these three to choose will often result in including the 'feeling' aspect more often than we would otherwise do.

Thirdly, there is our manner and delivery. We don't get to hear people speaking in Scripture in terms of their tone of voice and so on, but the prophets, Jesus and the apostles use emotive language at times, and we're sometimes told of their feelings as they spoke.

We need to develop in ourselves the appropriate emotional attitude for what we are speaking about, and then allow it to show itself as we speak. Our different personalities will mean that this looks different for each of us, but I presume our congregations shouldn't be left unsure as to what we feel about the topic, just as they shouldn't be unsure as to what we have said about it.

This is clearly not something to be worked up artificially – and we should beware of any kind of pretence. In his lectures to students, Spurgeon warned against pretence in the pulpit. He said, 'Be earnest and you will seem to be earnest. A burning heart will soon find for itself a flaming tongue.'[3]

Spurgeon's challenge then was for authenticity: to cultivate the appropriate heart feelings which would then naturally show themselves in speech. The challenge for me is to get a burning heart, which will show itself in a flaming tongue.

Richard Baxter said that one of our aims in preaching for our listeners is 'to warm their hearts by kindling in them holy affections, as by a communication from ours'.[4] But that means that our own affections must be warmed first, and they must be demonstrated as we speak.

Obviously we should also beware of emotional manipulation from the pulpit. Some of us may be good orators who can stir people: we know how to tell a story, use an illustration, and so on. We can have people laughing, crying and then laughing again. People can feel very moved. But unless the connections have been made with knowledge, they won't know why they feel moved. There might be great feeling, but it has no foundation. And so it won't last, and it is inappropriate in itself.

5. Our care of people

We've seen examples in Scripture of feelings expressed from leaders to people they care for:

- Paul expresses his great love for the Philippians whom he longs for with the affection of Christ Jesus (Philippians 1:7–8)
- Paul express his great concern and exasperation with the Galatians who he is in 'the pains of childbirth' over (Galatians 4:19–20)
- Paul expresses his daily concern for all the churches (2 Corinthians 11:28)
- John says he has great joy to know that his 'children' are walking in the truth (2 John 4)

The point is that we should express how we feel towards the people we care for. We will do that in different ways depending on our own personalities, and we will vary it depending on who the recipient is and depending on their personality. But people should know we love them, are worried for them, cry over them, or whatever is appropriate, given what is going on in their lives.

It is also pastorally useful to address people's feelings. As we care for individuals, they will be telling us they feel happy or sad, confident or unsure, and so on. We should pick up on these feelings and gently help them to know why they are feeling that way. What heart values lie behind those feelings? Or in addressing an issue, we will ask, 'How do you feel about that?' In this way, feelings can help us in getting to the root of the issue.

We must also appreciate the motivational power of our emotions. We often see people who know the right thing, but struggle to live it out. They know pornography is wrong, but look at it; they know satisfaction doesn't lie in possessions, but chase them anyway; they know they shouldn't envy others, but find themselves doing so.

Here again, we need to make sure we include feelings in our ministry to people. We need not only to help them see that something is wrong so they understand they shouldn't do it, but also help them change their heart so that they hate what is wrong and love what is good.

Isaac Watts said, 'Even where reason is bright and the judgement clear, yet it will be ineffectual for any valuable purposes, if religion reach no farther than the head, and proceed not to the heart: it will have but little influence if there are none of the affections engaged.'[5] The right emotional engagement is often what is missing in our fight for holiness.

In all these ways and others, I hope that bringing the aspect of our feelings to bear will help both us and those we serve in ministry.

recommended further reading

Brian S. Borgman, *Feelings and Faith: Cultivating Godly Emotions in the Christian Life* (Crossway, 2009).

Tim Chester, *You Can Change: God's Transforming Power for Our Sinful Behaviour and Negative Emotions* (IVP, 2008).

Jonathan Edwards, *The Religious Affections* (Banner of Truth, 1961).

Matthew Elliott, *Faithful Feelings: Emotion in the New Testament* (IVP, 2005).

Marjory F. Foyle, *Honourably Wounded: Stress among Christian Workers* (Monarch, 2009).

Dennis P. Hollinger, *Head, Heart and Hands: Bringing Together Christian Thought, Passion and Action* (IVP, 2005).

Michael P. Jensen (ed.), *True Feelings: Perspectives on Emotions in Christian Life and Ministry* (IVP: forthcoming publication, 2012).

Timothy S. Lane and Paul David Tripp, *How People Change* (New Growth Press, 2006).

Joni Eareckson Tada, *A Place of Healing: Wrestling with the Mysteries of Suffering, Pain, and God's Sovereignty* (David C. Cook, 2010).

Edward T. Welch, *Depression: A Stubborn Darkness – Light for the Path* (New Growth Press, 2004).

notes

Chapter 1 Approaching emotions

1. D. Martyn Lloyd-Jones, *Spiritual Depression: Its Causes and Cures* (Pickering and Inglis, 1965), p. 109.
2. D. A. Carson, *Love in Hard Places* (Crossway, 2002), p. 21.

Chapter 2 What do perfect emotions look like?

1. B. B. Warfield, 'The Emotional Life of Our Lord', *The Person and Work of Christ* (P&R Publishing, 1950), pp. 141–142.
2. John Calvin, *Commentary on John's Gospel*, Crossway Classic Commentaries (Crossway, 1994), p. 279.
3. Calvin, *Commentary on John*, p. 280.
4. David Powlison, *Seeing with New Eyes: Counseling and the Human Condition Through the Lens of Scripture* (P&R Publishing, 2003), p. 218.

Chapter 3 Getting to the heart of emotions

1. Jonathan Edwards, *Religious Affections*, Works of Jonathan Edwards, vol. 2 (Yale University Press, 1959), p. 95.

2. Edwards, *Religious Affections*, p. 119.
3. Augustine, *City of God* (CUP, 1998), IX.5.365.
4. Thomas Boston, *Human Nature in Its Fourfold State* (Banner of Truth, 1964), p. 127.
5. John Calvin, *Commentary on John's Gospel*, Crossway Classic Commentaries (Crossway, 1994), p. 280.
6. Augustine, *City of God*, XIV.8.592.

Chapter 5 Putting emotions in their right place

1. Thomas Goodwin, *The Vanity of Thoughts*, http://www.monergism.com/directory/link_category/Puritans/Thomas-Goodwin/.
2. John Wesley, *Letters*, ed. John Telford (Epworth Press, 1931), vol. 8, p. 190.
3. Jonathan Edwards, *Religious Affections*, Works of Jonathan Edwards, vol. 2 (Yale University Press, 1959), p. 251.

Chapter 6 Emotions and the Bible

1. Richard Baxter, *The Saints' Everlasting Rest*, Practical Works of Richard Baxter, vol. 3 (Soli Deo Gloria Publications, 2000), p. 306.

Chapter 7 Emotions and God's praise

1. Isaac Watts, *The Psalms of David*, Works of Isaac Watts, vol. 4 (Longman et al., London, 1753), p. xiv.
2. Jonathan Edwards, *Religious Affections*, Works of Jonathan Edwards, vol. 2 (Yale University Press, Yale, 1959), p. 115.
3. John Calvin, *Institutes of the Christian Religion*, trans. F. L. Battles (SCM, 1961), III.20.32, p. 895.
4. Bob Kauflin, *Worship Matters: Leading Others to Encounter the Greatness of God* (Crossway, 2008), p. 139.
5. Edwards, *Religious Affections*, p. 266.

Chapter 9 Feeling down

1. Carl Trueman, *The Wages of Spin: Critical Writings on Historical and Contemporary Evangelicalism* (Christian Focus, 2007).
2. David Powlison, *Seeing with New Eyes: Counseling and the Human Condition Through the Lens of Scripture* (P&R Publishing, 2003), p. 221.
3. D. Martyn Lloyd-Jones, *Spiritual Depression: Its Causes and Cures* (Pickering and Inglis, 1965), pp. 20–21.
4. Edward T. Welch, *Depression: A Stubborn Darkness* (New Growth Press, 2004), pp. 20–25.
5. C. H. Spurgeon, *Lectures to My Students*, series 1, lecture 11 (Baker, 1977), pp. 167, 179.

Chapter 10 Knowing what to expect and facing the future

1. Isaac Watts, *The Doctrine of the Passions*, Works of Isaac Watts, vol. 2 (Longman et al., London, 1753), p. 628.

Appendix: A note to those in Christian ministry

1. D. B. Knox, *Sent by Jesus: Some Aspects of Christian Ministry Today* (Banner of Truth, 1992), p. 73.
2. Jonathan Edwards, *Religious Affections*, Works of Jonathan Edwards, vol. 2 (Yale University Press, 1959), p. 116.
3. C. H. Spurgeon, *Lectures to My Students*, series 2, lecture 8, (Baker, 1977), p. 148.
4. Richard Baxter, *The Reformed Pastor* (Banner of Truth, 1974), p. 50.
5. Isaac Watts, *The Love of God*, Works of Isaac Watts, vol. 2 (Longman et al., 1753), p. 663.

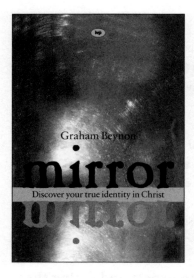

also by Graham Beynon

Mirror, Mirror
Discover your true identity in Christ
Graham Beynon

ISBN: 9781844743254
160 pages, paperback

Our identity or self-image is a bit like looking in a mirror.
We see our reflection and make judgments about ourselves.
However, the 'mirror' we use tends to be the world around us,
rather than the one we should use.

James 1:23–24 tells us that the Bible, God's word, is like a
mirror. We look into it and see what we are really like. The
world tells us that we need a good self-image. The Bible says
that we need a right self-image.

In *Mirror, Mirror*, Graham Beynon helps us realign our thinking.

*'Excellent. Thoroughly contemporary. Thoroughly biblical. And
the intersection of the two is mind-blowing. In a day when
Christians so often simply baptize the latest trends in secular
psychology, this book is refreshingly biblical, genuinely life-
changing, a great model of Christian thinking. Here is the word
of God reviving the soul. Here is good news. Here is freedom.'*
Tim Chester

Available from your local Christian bookshop or **www.thinkivp.com**

also by Graham Beynon

Last Things First
Living in the light of the future
Graham Beynon

ISBN: 9781844744121
176 pages, paperback

Why think about the future? After all, it only leads to controversy and it's irrelevant to life now ...

However, Graham Beynon shows that the real danger is that we don't think about the future. God in his Word puts last things first - the whole gospel is shaped around what is to come. God has a plan for where he is taking this world, and his people are called to live in the light of that future.

The Bible teaches Christians to store up treasure in heaven; to wait faithfully for the return of their Master; to think of this world as temporary and passing; and to think of the world to come as their inheritance.

Graham Beynon takes a fresh look at this teaching and shows how what is to come should shape practical Christian living now, with regard to godliness, handling of money, service of others, speaking about Jesus, faithfulness to him, response to hardship, and more.

Available from your local Christian bookshop or **www.thinkivp.com**

also by Graham Beynon

God's New Community
New Testament patterns for today's church
Graham Beynon

ISBN: 9781844744817
144 pages, paperback

When someone uses the word 'church', what comes into your mind? A building where a congregation meets? A room inside such a building? The main Sunday meeting? A denomination?

Graham Beynon shows that when the Bible talks about 'church', it is always only referring to people, and a particular sort of people at that. From a range of key passages in the New Testament, he explains what church is, what it is for, how it is to work, how it is to be led, and what it means to belong to God's new community in Christ.

'... faithful to Scripture, well illustrated, and helpfully applied.'
Evangelical Times

'This challenging book is a thought-provoking exploration of what it means to be part of the church.' Evangelicals Now

'This clear, simple, biblical and practical guide will deepen your understanding and enrich your experience of church.'
Julian Hardyman

also by Graham Beynon

Experiencing the Spirit
New Testament essentials for every Christian
Graham Beynon

ISBN: 9781844744800
160 pages, paperback

For some Christians, God the Holy Spirit is something of a mystery, and they are not too sure what to say about him. Others speak with confidence and enthusiasm about him, challenging us to be 'filled with the Spirit', or to live a 'Spirit-filled life'. As a result, the work of the Spirit has sometimes been controversial.

Graham Beynon looks at the main New Testament passages in which the Spirit's work is described. With freshness and clarity, he builds a picture of what the Holy Spirit does, and hence what experiencing him in our lives should look like.

'The Holy Spirit is both essential and often misunderstood. Here is a book that is biblically accurate, simply expressed and well illustrated. I'll be recommending it to my own congregation and I am happy now to commend it to you.' Mark Dever

Available from your local Christian bookshop or **www.thinkivp.com**

discover more great Christian books
at www.ivpbooks.com

Full details of all the books from Inter-Varsity Press – including reader reviews, author information, videos and free downloads – are available on our website at **www.ivpbooks.com**.

IVP publishes a wide range of books on various subjects including:

Biography

Christian Living

Bible Studies

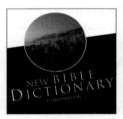

Reference

Commentaries

Theology

On the website you can also sign up for regular email newsletters, tell others what you think about books you have read by posting reviews, and locate your nearest Christian bookshop using the *Find a Store* feature.